TH

WE

OI

GRIEF

The Web of Grief

Copyright © 2019 Rhiannon M. Jones

ISBN 9781792871993

For Deeday
from Rhi. Ann. On.

Acknowledgements

Firstly, I have to thank my mum and dad, for being the best human beings in the world and giving me and David unconditional love, an amazing life, wonderful memories, morals, two superhuman role models and two amazing parents, which grew into our friends. You guys are far from normal, but why would we want normal, when we could have the best?

A massive thank you to my husband, Jamie, who I would absolutely not have coped without during this journey, for being patient, loving and kind to me during my highs but especially during my lows. For being a shoulder (as well as a tissue) for me to cry on, for holding me and knowing exactly what I needed even when I didn't know myself. You're my favourite.

To my three children, Dane, Jae and Casey for giving me purpose and keeping me going. For making me laugh and smile even when I didn't want to, for putting my life into perspective, for always loving, helping and looking after me. I love you, boys!

To my amazing friend, Danielle, who has been such a positive influence to me and exactly what I needed. I truly believe that you were sent to me for a reason and I am so grateful for you helping me to focus on the amazing possibilities of the future. Thank you for your support with everything I dream about, especially this book. Gracias, Amiga.

To Faye, for being a massive support on the most difficult night of my life, and acting like it didn't mess up all of your plans, and for being a support and good friend every day since. Neither of us knew what was about to happen, but your kindness was inspiring and so appreciative. I don't think I will ever find words to justify how grateful I am to you.

To all my friends and family, for being there for all of us and uniting, ready for when we gained the strength to reach out.

And lastly, but mostly, Thank you to my big brother, David, for always making me laugh, for our deep conversations, for being my friend and even for always teasing and laughing at me and fighting with me when we were younger, because now, I have so many amazing memories with you and I hold them so dearly. You always listened to me when I needed to talk, and now you have no choice but to listen because I talk to you all the time. You are such a selfless and wonderful soul and you are still guiding me and giving me little messages as well as feeding your insults to me so I know that our bond isn't broken. It makes me happy. I didn't tell you enough when I had the chance, but I really do love you.

Introduction

My brother's surprise passing left my whole family in complete shock. We were fortunate enough to have each others support and love but every single day was a conscious and continuous struggle.

Although I had experienced grief previously, this particular time knocked me off my feet. Silently, I was caught in a web of grief and wasn't honest about how I was coping to those closest to me. The more I struggled inside, the more tangled I got. The more tangled I got, the more I tried to kick and wriggle myself free but to no avail.

I desperately tried to find ways to cope and to find information on situations similar to mine, but I couldn't. I was regularly met with the same old: "*Time's a healer.*" When I read people's stories about grief, none seemed to relate to mine. I just wanted to know what helped someone that had been through something like me so they could offer some help or advice. I had no luck and had to go it alone. This book is about the sides of grief (and healing) that no one really talks about and how I released the shackles of the sticky web of grief.

In this book, I get extremely honest and raw about what I went through internally and externally and the methods I used to help me to deal with how difficult daily life became. It was important for me to be honest and share my story so that I could metaphorically stand beside those who can relate and tell them "*you can do this!*"

I cannot tell anyone how to feel or what they are going through. We are all so different and process the world we live in differently. I can only tell you about my journey and what I found to be true about grief from my perspective. Let's all take one day, one hour, one minute at a time and allow ourselves the time and space for our individual journeys. This is mine...

Chapter 1
Friday 13th

"If you're going through hell - keep going."
-Winston Churchill

It's ironic that this is where my story starts, as it's the last chapter that I wanted to write. I guess it's also a bit poetic that I have now come full circle again and completed the cycle. Throughout this whole book, I knew this would be the most difficult chapter to write. I have cried a lot throughout the process of writing this book, but this chapter is the most difficult part for me to relive and revisit. I kept writing, editing, adding to other chapters and still left this one looming in the background, waiting patiently to be acknowledged. I guess that's how grief can be to a lot of people. You can try to drown out the nagging voice in your head or numb the pain you don't want to feel, but it's useless because you can't avoid the inevitable, and no matter how much I tried to busy myself with other chapters, this one sat there waiting and knowing that I'd have to write it if I wanted to finish my book. *Smug little chapter!*

Friday, 13th October 2017, started like any normal day. I went for a run (I make it sound like I'm really active but I'm really not) and I only know this because I took a picture whilst I was out on my run. I do actually remember having a weird feeling during my run. It wasn't a feeling of dread or a sick feeling telling me something bad was going to happen and I'm not for one minute claiming I knew what was going to happen, but something was off, and I couldn't get into my run that day. I shook it off and cannot remember anything else until me and Casey, my youngest, went to collect my other two children, Dane and Jae from school. Dane also arranged for a friend to come over for a sleepover. My husband, Jamie had told me he was working late but luckily, we have good kids and they were all playing nicely so it wasn't a problem.

I remember Dane's friend's mum, Faye, coming to drop off his bag for the sleepover. We had a little chat but she had her other son's friend staying at her house, so she went on her way. I have no recollection of the time. I would guess it was around 6pm but it was seconds after I shut the door to her my phone started to ring. Dane, his friend and Jae were all upstairs playing and Casey was in the living room with me. I looked at my phone and it was my dad calling. I'm one of the lucky people in this world to adore my parents and happy as ever to hear from him, I cheerily answered the phone "Hi pop!"
Those were the last words I ever said before the world as I knew it collapsed around me. The last words I ever said in ignorant bliss.
My dad's reply was urgent and desperate, he was crying and just told me that mum isn't answering her phone and to go and get her from bingo then to come to their house. I tried to keep him calm, agreed that I would but asked him to tell me what the matter was. Dad wouldn't tell me over the phone but pleaded that I go and get mum then bring her home. There was nothing else I could do but to agree.
My mind was racing. *What the hell*? I have never got a phone call like that before from my mum or dad, so I

know that this had to be big. He was hurting and desperate. I knew that nothing was wrong with my mum, as she was oblivious to it all. It couldn't be about him as he was phoning. It can't be about David, my brother, he's only 30. Is it my Nan or Grandad? My mind was on overload at this point.

Ok, think! I am alone in a house with four children. My mum and dad's house is about a 10 minute drive away and Jamie has the car. I can get a cab, that's not a problem, but there are four children here aged seven and younger and by the sounds of it, something big and upsetting has happened, so I don't think I should take them with me. If I call Jamie, it's going to take him a good hour to get home and that's *if* he doesn't get stuck in Friday night traffic. I need to be at my dad's house, like… **now**! We only moved here two years ago and don't know many people in the area.
Think…
Think!
Faye had just left. I quickly phoned her and vaguely told her about my dad's phone call, that he was crying and I had no idea what was happening. I asked her if she would mind coming back to sit with the boys while I went to see what was happening. I told her that her other son and his friend were welcome to come in and use and abuse the house. She instantly agreed and was at my door within minutes. In the meantime, I had quickly put Casey to bed, and I mean *quickly!* I was running around my house like a mad woman. I had no concept of time during this all. I don't know how long it all took; it felt like about 5 minutes from when I got the phone call to being in the cab.

Just before I left, my dad had phoned back and said, in a slightly, calmer tone, that *they* had gone to get mum so I should just come straight to him. I had no idea who '*they*' were, and I wasn't going to ask. I told my dad I was on my way and would be there soon but again, asked him what was wrong. The pain returned in his voice and he refused to tell me on the phone. I found out later, that my dad assumed Jamie was home and I had the car (and of course I didn't tell him I was home alone and not only had to get the cab but had to get someone to look after my children) so he didn't want to tell me, upset me and for me to have an accident in the car, racing over to his house.

It's funny, normally, when you're in a rush to be somewhere; it seems to take forever to get there. Yet this cab ride, felt like I practically teleported to my mum and dad's house. I don't know if I blacked out or some mystical force knew that I had to be there ASAP but time seemed to go quickly.
As the cab turned onto my mum and dad's road, I knew I was about to walk into something crazy. My dad doesn't just phone me crying! As we approached their house, I saw an ambulance car outside and my heart dropped. My cab fare came to about £8 but I threw £20 (the only cash I had) at the driver and ran out the car to their house because money was of no importance. I literally did not care.

The street door was open and I ran inside shouting for my dad. I ran into the living room and was vaguely aware that there was someone sitting at the dining table, but again, everything was unimportant. I just needed to get to my dad. I saw him stand up from the sofa so I ran to him and put my arms around him asking him what happened.

My sweet, loving dad broke down. In between sobs I heard the words "David's dead".

I was stunned, and the world started to swirl around me. My brother is... *dead*? My dad and I embracing each other as he was trying to relive the horror that he had just experienced. I think he felt both relieved and guilty when he was telling me. My poor dad had been dealing with this all alone until I arrived, and then he erupted when I stormed through the door.

Just a normal Friday night, mum goes off to bingo after work. Dad buys a pizza on his way home from work. David works shifts so if he's not working, he normally shares a pizza with dad. My dad got home and knocked on David's bedroom door to see if he wanted some pizza. There was no answer, so my dad went in and saw David lying on his bed. David didn't respond and was cold, and my dad knew. He phoned emergency services and the ambulance staff arrived fairly quickly. One of them was sitting at the table when I arrived, the other had gone to get my mum. They were both amazing.

David was 30 years old and completely healthy. To say this was unexpected is a huge understatement.

My dad was trying his best to explain but still couldn't make sense of it himself. I had so many questions but knew that my dad was suffering as it was.

My poor mum. She doesn't even know yet.

The ambulance staff say that there are no signs that he suffered, that they believe it is something to do with his heart, that it looks as though he went in his sleep as he was peacefully tucked up in bed and that he probably didn't even know what was happening to him.

I remember begging and pleading that they were right. *Don't let him have suffered. I hope he wasn't scared.* They see things like this all the time, they're professionals, they know what they're talking about, don't they?

My dad breaking down in front of my eyes like that shocked me. It shocked me into action. I knew that I had to do everything I could to be there for him.

Not long after, I heard someone enter the house and knew my mum was home. This was awful. My mum is such a strong woman and I saw the look in her eyes, just searching for my dad, longing to be held. Longing to be told it wasn't true.

The ambulance lady had broken the news to my mum and luckily she was with her best friend so was supported all the way home. Seeing my mum and dad hold each other like that was both beautiful and extremely painful. My dad then had to retell the story to my mum. My mum's friend hugged my dad and then me, but I remember feeling absent. Like part of my mind was somewhere completely different. Then I remembered my kids. And Jamie. I went to the garden to make these phone calls. I knew I couldn't say it out loud in front of my mum and dad. I wasn't even sure if I could say it out loud at all.

First, I called Jamie. I tried to follow the wise footsteps of my dad and I told myself I wasn't going to tell him exactly what had happened, I was going to stay calm and just tell him to come to my mum and dad's house because I didn't want him to rush over and get in an accident in all the panic. Except, as soon as I heard his voice as he answered the phone, I vomited the ugly truth down the phone. I didn't mean to, it just spat out of my mouth and I just needed him here with me. And just like that, he was on his way.

Next, I had to phone Faye. I had no idea how long it had been since I left her at my house, but the last she had heard, my dad phoned me in tears and then I ran out the door. So, I phoned her and briefly filled her in. She was so lovely, she told me they were all fine and that I should take my time and there was no rush. I don't know if she knows, or if I'll ever be able to express how truly amazing and invaluable she was that night.

Obviously, the ambulance staff had to call the police due to the suddeness of David's death. They assured us they were not treating it as suspicious, that it's just a formality and we completely understood. As far as I was concerned, anyone who could potentially give us some answers, were welcome.

In the meantime, the ambulance staff gave us as much information as they could (which wasn't a lot) and tried to support us as best they could offering advice and comfort with their words.

We really came together as a family and were all comforting and supporting each other, but I felt so guilty that we were all downstairs together, and David was upstairs all alone. I had asked to see him earlier, and they said I could, just after they had done their checks. When they were ready, they told me I could go and see him. I wanted to, I needed to, but I was scared. Of what? I don't know. I was never scared of David when he was alive, so I don't know why I was scared now. Maybe I didn't want it to be true. Maybe it was so far from anything I thought that I would want to do, I never thought I would want to see a dead body, but this was my brother!

We all stood up to go and see him and say goodbye as the private ambulance was on their way to collect his body. Halfway to the door, my mum said she couldn't do it and didn't want to see him like that and started crying again. I completely understood and now that I look back, I'm glad she didn't come in because as I saw him lying on the bed, looking vaguely familiar, I knew he wasn't David. Previously, I never understood when people would say: "*she just wasn't there anymore*", but that's exactly how it was. The soul, the life, had drained from his body and there was just a shell on the bed. The real David was somewhere else, probably eating some good food or chilling with a book and a whiskey. It wasn't a nice memory, but now, I'm glad I saw him so that I could see that he was gone and there was no way I could deny it. By the time we went to see him in the chapel of rest, my mum included, the funeral home had done a fantastic job and he looked more like his usual self. He looked as though he was sleeping.

When they came to take David, I was trying my best to support my mum and dad. By now, Jamie had arrived and I had my husband to support me, so I could support my mum and dad. As I saw them leave with David, I wanted to scream. To run after them and take him back. It felt so final. So…. wrong. He belonged here with his family. But I tried my hardest not to let my emotions show, to be strong for my parents.

The policeman had checked David and his room over by now for any evidence to help find out what had happened, then, he wanted to speak with us to see what happened and if we could offer any help to understand how a healthy young man of 30-years-old was found lifeless in his bed.

He was really nice and sympathetic to our feelings, but it was still unpleasant. The kind of questions he asked weren't relevant here. David didn't have any enemies and was not interested in fighting or taking drugs, so why him?

When everyone had left and we had sorted out all we could, my mum and dad told me and Jamie to go home to the boys. I didn't want to leave, but they insisted, so we left but I had never felt such guilt and sickness in my stomach. I didn't want to stay there, I did want to go home, but leaving them made me feel disgusting. Jamie took me home and everything felt so surreal.

We got back and explained a little more to Faye what had happened and thanked her for absolutely everything. She left with her boys and Jamie went up to put our boys to bed after a fun and exciting night they'd had with Faye. We had agreed to not tell the boys just yet. Jamie had asked his mum to have them for the weekend so they were away from the chaos and so that we could get to grips a little more.

That night, I don't know how much sleep I got, I just remember asking Jamie to cling to my side as I didn't want to be alone. I was numb. Dumfounded.

I suggested that no one else was told until tomorrow. It was already late and there was nothing anyone could have done at that hour, I thought *let them get some sleep because tomorrow they're going to get some awful news.*

I told my mum and dad that I would go to tell my nan and grandad first thing in the morning. So, on his way to take the boys to his mum's, Jamie dropped me off at my nan and grandad's house. My dad thought someone should go and tell them in person to make sure they were supported.

I was still in shock and still not allowing myself to feel much. I had to be strong but saying out loud the painful and still unbelievable truth made me feel like a disgusting human being. I knew what I was saying was true but how could I say this to people that I love knowing that it would crush them? I had to keep composed as much as I could to give them all the information that I had in a clear way so that it didn't come out as a blubbering mess.

My nan, bless her, can't always hear very well and she could see me getting upset as I was talking and asked my grandad what I said, I then sat there and watched him repeat to my nan what I had just told them. I had to watch her heart break as his words cut right through her. My poor grandad being the same bad news bearer as I was.

It felt like a sick joke as the words left my mouth. Who the hell did I think I was? Did people think it was like a twisted way for me to get attention? Because the truth was surely not an option.

David?

Died?

How?!
In his sleep?

Looking back, it's touching to see how many people supported all of us, but in particular, my mum and dad. We had a crazy and tough road ahead of us and the love and support we received was really helpful. Not only were we shocked and in disbelief but we also had so many questions. I remember waking up at times and just for a few glorious seconds, forgot reality. I was in ignorant bliss that anything was wrong or different but then the realisation instantly wound around me and lured me into that dark place. We had so many questions, too many questions. Most of which would not be answered for a long time. The biggest one was 'How did this happen?' How did a 30-year-old young man with no health issues stop breathing in his sleep? We know he must have been sleeping as he was lying in bed under his duvet but the rest I could not comprehend.

David was sent for a post-mortem which isn't a nice feeling knowing what they would do to my brother but we knew they have to and we needed answers too. Waiting to know why or get some sort of clarity was torture. Every time the phone would ring, I was hoping we would hear something. Waiting around offered no help to my peace of mind. I feared going to sleep. I feared every time I put my kids to bed, it would be the last time. I created so much drama in my head that I became irrational internally. Externally, I was very logical and saying what I believed to be all the right things but I wasn't being honest with myself, so it created a tug of war effect. It was exhausting.

When we finally got the phone call from the coroner's office, we were told that his post-mortem came back inconclusive.

"*What does that mean?*" I asked my dad.

"It means they couldn't find out what happened" his reply and the realisation of it all was crushing. We had questions that needed answering. Why did this happen?

They told us they were going to do a second post-mortem and it wasn't long before they released his body so that we could proceed with funeral arrangements. I guess they would look over the information that was already recorded to do the second post-mortem. Although I was desperate, I wasn't hopeful.

My mum and dad were amazing through everything, including the funeral process. They gave me an open invitation to everything so that I could attend what I wanted and when I wanted but when I needed space to breathe, that was fine too. They told me every appointment, every meeting, *everything*. They made it clear that I was welcome but that I shouldn't feel obliged. They are the most amazing people.

My brother's funeral was a very difficult day for me, as you can imagine, but I also felt a lot of unexpected emotions. The service was really well articulated and everyone commented to say it did David justice. The hall was packed, which speaks volumes and is a huge compliment to David. A lot of people came back to my mum and dad's house for the wake and I remember being stopped in my tracks. I was walking around and all I could hear was people deep in conversation sharing their stories and memories of David. Each captured one of his amazing and unique qualities and the energy in the room was magnetic. I was so overwhelmed with love and appreciation for my brother and seeing so many people who were touched and blessed to have known him was truly beautiful. It's a feeling that I am so grateful for. I went home that night feeling a lot lighter and freer than I had done in weeks.

When the day came that we finally got some information from David's post-mortem, it was a bittersweet time. We were told that David, unknowingly, had an enlarged heart and that it just stopped working while he was sleeping. Obviously, we were all beating ourselves up with shoulda, woulda, couldas but in reality, none of us were to know, not even him. The torment wasn't over yet though. We found out that some types of enlarged hearts can be hereditary so my mum, dad and I all had to be tested. Jamie and I agreed that I would be tested and then we would go from there to see if the boys had to be tested too as we didn't want them to go through a scary or unnecessary experience if they didn't need to. They had been through enough. My dad was also getting really light headed and even having blackouts at this time, so it was a really scary and daunting time for all of us.

In hindsight, it probably wasn't that long before we all got our results, but when you've been told you may have the same health issue from which your brother/son has died, every day feels like a week. You start to question the safety and risks of everyday tasks in case they do some damage that you had never contemplated previously. Luckily enough, all our results came back clear and it was one less thing for us to worry about and to let go of.

It was, without a doubt, the most difficult time of our lives and something that we had never considered that we would have had to encounter. It was sudden, unexpected and has been a continuous journey ever since. Some days we have more strength than others but every day is an adjustment.

In this book, I tell my struggles and another side of grief about which no one ever told me about in the hope that, should you ever need it, for bereavement, grief or for life in general, that you find something that helps you see the light at the other end. So that you can release the sticky web that's holding you back and free yourself. And believe me, you **can** get safely through to the other side. What does freedom feel like to you?

Chapter 2
Grief

"Grief, I've learned, is really just love. It's all the love you want to give but cannot. All of that unspent love gathers up in the corners of your eyes, the lump in your throat, and in the hollow part of your chest. Grief is just love with no place to go."

-Unknown

Like most words and phrases in our language, we overuse them so much that we devalue them. "*I love you*", "*Words cannot describe*" and "*exhausted*" are a few that spring to my mind. When we really think about them and their meaning, they are so much more powerful than we realise because they're regularly overused on a daily basis in an off-the-cuff remark. This is what grief is like for me.

We know that people grieve. We also know that people can grieve after all different circumstances. The most obvious is to grieve after a bereavement, but you can also grieve the loss of a relationship (romantic, friendship or professional), after a big life change like moving home, city or to a new job that isn't living up to expectation. You can grieve the 'loss' of your youth if you're particularly attached to numbers and ages that you feel define part of your identity. You can grieve after your favourite band has split. You can even grieve the end of a television, film or book series that you have become so engrossed and invested in that you question how you will ever not know what happens next. Or is that just me?

My point is, grief comes in so many different ways into our life. The strongest, to me, is after bereavement. The least painful (but still upsetting) is as I take the last bite of a rich and creamy delicious cheesecake knowing that there is no more. *Yes, I grieve the end of food. Don't judge me.* I'm not comparing one against the other because they are completely different. Just like I can be happy to sit down and enjoy a film with my family after a long and stressful day and I can also be happy to win the lottery. You can't compare one to the other because they're both so different.

What we also have to remember is that our emotions do not have one level. For example, every time I think about yoga, I am not energetic and excited. Sometimes I just want to go to sleep as I'm shattered and only want to read in bed before I crash out after 25 seconds. Other times, I have so much energy and cannot wait to roll out my mat and start stretching my body while listening to relaxing music, or '*humming music*' as my children call it. Yoga doesn't trigger one emotion at one frequency in me, it differs. It also differs between different people. You might be so excited to do yoga all day every day. You might groan in boredom by the thought of it. That's ok.

Grief is the same. Some days it is more painful than others. Some days I literally just want to curl up in some comfy PJs with a big blanket around me and feel sorry for myself all day while I cry at my loss. Other days I'm so motivated and determined to live my absolute best life so that I can live for both my brother and myself. In my opinion, both are grieving because they are both a reaction to the loss I'm experiencing. This is why it is so important to not judge people in their grieving process, because let me tell you, the grief process is confusing, conflicting and oh so exhausting to whoever is going through it. Watching TV and films, I have often heard about the seven steps of grief which are:

1. Shock
2. Denial
3. Pain
4. Anger
5. Bargaining
6. Depression
7. Acceptance/Hope

Now, I don't know if I'm the only one here, but I always took it to be like a system. For example, initially you experience shock, after some time you then progress into the second step, denial. You spend some time in this step and then you progress into the third step, pain. You continue along all the steps dealing with whatever you need to deal with until you've completed all the steps all the way to step seven and have accepted it. *Congratulations! You're healed.*

Except... that's not really how things work. These stages are definitely all part of the process and I guess it's good to have a reference, if that's your thing, but what no one tells you is that you can experience all seven of these steps in one day, and not necessarily in that order. It truly is like going one step forward then two steps back. Then three steps forward. Then five back. Then two forward. It's almost like a sad and unfamiliar dance you go through and you just can't quite get the hang of the rhythm, then when you think you've got it, the melody changes and you're disorientated again.

If you've ever been to a Zumba class, you might understand what I mean here and before you become outraged that grief could be compared to Zumba, bear with me. In my first Zumba class I didn't have a clue what I was doing. Everyone else around me knew the moves, knew the rhythm and was dancing along smiling and happy. Then there was me standing at the back with my mum, trying desperately to keep up, red-faced, gasping for water and air and secretly pleading to any god that would listen to make the next hour go so fast or at least to sound the fire alarm or something just so I could go home and it would all be over. I left that class feeling totally exhausted, deflated and didn't think I would ever get the hang of it. But stubborn as I am (and mainly because my mum made me) we went for the next few weeks and, slowly but surely, I began to get into the swing of things, learned a few moves, stopped less and less for some water and to catch my breath and even started to enjoy it.

This is how grief has been for me, and how I believe it is for most people. At first, you are totally overwhelmed and see everyone else smiling and enjoying life and you're just watching the world operate as if you're not really part of it, struggling to put one foot in front of the other. You can't ever imagine getting past the week let alone to a time when you can be happy and 'normal' ever again. But you take things day by day and as the days turn into weeks and weeks into months, you learn all the things you need to about yourself and deal with all the things you need to deal with. You become stronger than you ever knew was possible and you start to have more good days than bad because slowly but surely, you've learned the dance moves to this new and current chapter in your life. You look at how far you've come and can't quite work out where or when things stopped being so overwhelming. Luckily though, you don't have to work it out or try to analyse or understand it, you just need to let it happen. Just do your best to get through each day and do all the things that make you feel better (including having a cry to release if you need to).

I think it's much easier to just ride the waves than to paddle against the tide.

I'm going to let you in on a secret. This could be a *loooong* and exhausting road ahead of you and you don't want to burn out too quickly. Don't apply pressure to yourself or have expectations of where you think you should be or compare yourself to where you think others are. You are going to have ups and downs and feel like you're going round and round in circles.

Take. Your. Time.

This is not a race. There is no rush. You're dealing with a major shift and change in your life here, and there is no rule book. You might even have a delay in your emotions and start grieving a little later, and that's ok too. You might notice that you've allowed yourself to go in a downward spiral to a low point and that's ok. You've observed it, acknowledged it, now forgive yourself and start again. It's never too late to change your actions, words or atmosphere to help yourself heal.

Recently, I was having a chat with a family friend, who happens to be an undertaker, about us losing David, and her losing her mum. We were talking about the grieving process and she said something that really became a lightbulb moment for me. She said something like this:

"*What I've realised, in my many years at my job, comforting people who are dealing with loss, and especially in my own experience, is that the words we need to get rid of are 'should', 'can' and 'need'. Too often we hear 'you should go for a walk', 'you need to get out for a bit', 'you shouldn't be doing the cleaning at a time like this' or 'you can't keep doing this to yourself' but it's all ridiculous. We all cope with grief differently and most of the time we don't even feel like we're 'coping' at all. We just do whatever we need to do to get through the day, especially in the early days of grief.*"

She was spot on. Although most of the time, people's words are coming from a place of love, it's important to be more mindful of the words we are saying and how it might affect people. What works for one person might not make someone else feel better. If you want to visit the cemetery of your loved one every morning and have a little chat and that's what makes you feel good and reinforces your bond, do it. If you can't bring yourself to see their headstone so you never go, don't go. If you want to keep the bedroom you shared with your loved one the same way it was before they died to remind you of your best years together, do it. If you want to change it to symbolise the change in your life or just give the room a new fresh feel, then do that.

There is no right or wrong. You also have to realise that just because you make a decision, it doesn't mean you can't decide something else later when you're in a different headspace. For example, initially, when my brother died, my mum wanted to scatter his ashes in her garden to keep him close and because he loved sitting in the garden with a drink and a good book. Although it wasn't what my dad and I wanted, we supported my mum and I told her that that's fine but she doesn't have to make any decisions at this early stage. Later, she changed her mind and decided to lay his ashes to rest in the cemetery where any family or friends could go and pay their respect whenever they wanted.

It comforts me knowing that I have somewhere special to go where I can physically make the effort to go and 'visit' my brother, have a little chat and some time to think. Other people want to keep their loved ones close and choose to bring their ashes home in an urn. Other people chose something else altogether. They're all different, none are right nor wrong.

One emotion that is not always talked about in relation to grief, is guilt. I experienced a lot of guilt during my grieving process but I think it's important to mention because we mainly associate grief with sadness and missing someone. Guilt is a normal reaction to loss. You may ask yourself (A.K.A. mentally bully yourself) with questions such as "Why did he have to die, and I get to live?"
"Why didn't I tell her how much she meant to me while she was still here?"
"Why did I pick fights about the most stupid things?" and

"How can I take my sons to my mum and dad's house when they've just lost their son?"
All of these can put you in a really bad place and that isn't really helping anyone. When you feel guilt creeping in, acknowledge it, and then ask yourself if you are to blame. If the answer is no, let it go. It doesn't help anyone, you may never get an answer and you definitely can't change the past.

For example,
"Why did he have to die, and I get to live?"
Am I to blame?
"No."
So, let it go.

If, however, the answer to that question is yes, then ask yourself if you can do something about it. If the answer is no, let it go, but more than likely the answer to this question is usually yes. For example,
"Why didn't I tell her how much she meant to me while she was still here?"
Am I to blame?
"Well, yes because I am responsible for my actions, although I didn't know better at the time and if I knew what the future held I would definitely have told her."
Can you do anything about it now?
"I guess I can still tell her, she might not be able to reply but I can tell her in a prayer or write her a letter expressing exactly how I feel."
OK good. Is there anything else you can do?
"I could tell her parents, her children or someone else that is close to her that would appreciate some kind words about her."
Good. Anything else?

"I guess I can learn from this and start to tell people I love them or I appreciate their friendship while I still have the chance to do it to their faces so that I'm not in this situation again with someone else and beating myself up for not appreciating what I have while I still have it."
Great!

This exercise only works if you tell the part of your mind that wants to feel sorry for itself and remain in 'poor me' mode (A.K.A. 'the ego') and get really, really honest with yourself. If it's too painful or you really can't find a positive, then you can wait a few hours, days, weeks or months and try it again. It's never too late to start allowing yourself to heal. Alternatively, you can ask a good friend to help you with the answers. Pick someone that is positive, supportive and has an open mind. Not a friend who will feel uncomfortable and suggest you ditch this 'feelings stuff' and go to the pub instead.

Another important point I really want to make here is that you don't have to deal with this all by yourself. There may be times when you just want to focus solely on yourself and try to process how you're feeling and that's completely fine. That's completely normal. But you don't have to maintain a certain image or character. Anyone can struggle with this, myself included, but we mainly see it with men. For some reason, we seem to be stuck in a really sexist stereotype of what men and women are. Women are emotional and it's socially acceptable to cry in front of family, friends or even strangers. But we have terrible phrases that suggest the opposite for men. Men are told to 'man up' and to 'grow a pair' at any sight of emotion. Let me be the first to say this is absolute bull poo! Although I believe there are definitely differences between men and women, we are all human beings. Humans are *emotional* beings. We are *physical* beings. Women need to express themselves and their emotions and they need a hug sometimes. They need to be touched and kissed and to feel, *physically and emotionally* loved and supported. Men are no different.

We all have different ways in which we express our love and we all have different ways in which make us feel loved, but we're not going to get into that now. My point is, it's so important to ask for help if you need it. Ask someone to get the kids from school, ask someone to help with the cleaning. Ask someone if you can pop in for a coffee and a chat. Don't be afraid. It shows real strength to ask for help. If, however, you're a stubborn old mule like me and really struggle to ask for help from even your nearest and dearest and it really pains you to be vulnerable and express how you feel, fear not! There are so many options we have living in this glorious technological age. You can:

- **Write.** You could try writing someone a letter (You can even burn it straight after) or just writing how you feel. Writing was probably the single most helpful thing I did that helped me. I found that just writing exactly how I felt in a notebook with nobody judging me, no faces staring at me with pity or dismissing how I felt. Just me releasing my thoughts onto a page. I would start writing not knowing what the hell I'm going to write, "I don't even know how I'm feeling" but I found that once I started, I couldn't stop. I would always have so much more clarity after writing and feel so much lighter. It doesn't matter how neat your handwriting is or how well you can spell, just get it all out of your head and onto the paper. I'd really recommend giving this a go. All you need is a pen or pencil and some scrap paper.

- **Read**. You could try reading self-development books to help you get to a more positive place. You could read a good fiction book to give you something else to focus on for a while. You could read online forums about people who have experienced a similar loss to you and what they did to get through. Whatever tickles your fancy.
- **Walk**. Or run. Or anything that gets you out in the fresh air that doesn't involve too much thinking. The idea is to get out in nature, get some fresh air in your lungs and allow your mind some space and freedom. I have found going for a walk to be amazing therapy. You can really just let go, question some things, explore thoughts and ideas and it can really help you gain some clarity and organise some mental chaos.
- **Speak**. Speak to friends, family, colleagues, or like I did finally after not knowing what else I could do, reach out to speak with a bereavement counsellor. This option suited me because I found it easier to speak to someone who I didn't know and who I never had to see again if I didn't want to. There are also so many amazing charities out there that would be more than happy to give you some more information about what they do and offer a

friendly ear or advice. Just because you don't know what to do or where to get help, it doesn't mean you never will. Just ask. Ask someone if they can recommend something or do a quick search online and you will be presented with a whole list of companies that were started to help people just like you and me.

- **Community**. You could search for a local support group to join where you can share your experience with people who have also experienced some of the things you have and who may be able to offer advice on things that have helped them. You could search for an online support group or social media community that offers support from people who know exactly how you're feeling. Sometimes people find the online community easier to express themselves as they are not face-to-face and do not need to uphold certain appearances.

- **Meditate.** This might seem pretty *out there* if you're new to meditation, but there's something to this, trust me. Meditation is not some magic trick that will take away your pain. This is going to be a journey, and although you want to get through to the other side as quickly as possible, it will take as long as it takes. That being said, meditation has been used for thousands of years by people from all different backgrounds to help them feel more connected, to a higher power, yes, but also to give clarity to problems or conflicts in their life that are being clouded by emotion and to help them see the bigger picture of their life or of life in general. And let's not forget, to feel peace, love and joy in their heart. I used to think words like this were closely followed by someone saying "*flower power*", but when you've felt it, you realise how truly special and beautiful that feeling is. There are plenty of free guided meditations online to help newbies. If there's a chance it *could* help you, surely it's worth a few minutes of your time.

Try all of these, some of them or something completely different that I haven't mentioned. I tried a few of these and found they didn't work for me, so I moved onto something else and when I found something that did work for me, it did make me feel better. Don't ever feel like you have no options because there is always an option. If your brain is too busy and you can't think of anything. Ask someone else, someone you know, an online community or ask a search engine. When the student is ready, the teacher will appear. What lights you up and makes you feel light as air?

Chapter 3
When the child becomes the Adult

"To care for those who once cared for us is one of the HIGHEST HONORS"
-Tia Walker, The inspired caregiver.

If you're one of the lucky ones, like me, to have wonderful childhood memories and actually enjoy being around your parents, you'd probably be at their side in a heartbeat, if need be. I hope it never comes to that, but in life, we all need support one way or another. Sometimes, we have a down day and just need a friendly ear to listen or we find ourselves in financial difficulty and support from friends and/or family can, literally, be life-saving. There are thousands of ways in which we might need someone's support one way or another.

When someone has been a constant rock of support, encouragement, love and laughter, like my parents have to me, you find yourself instantaneously at their side to catch them if they fall. Not because you want to save the day or to even the score, well not for me at least. For me, it was more through fear and I didn't know what else to do.

My dad, to me at least, is the true meaning of a man. He is someone who is there for his family, financially, emotionally, and physically. He isn't confined to anyone's opinions, expectations or stereotypes. He is unapologetically himself. He gives love freely and unconditionally and gave me the healthiest example (and highest standard) for what to expect in a partner and a man.

My mum is a modern-day badass wonder woman! She will not sit quietly in a corner and let anyone take liberties with her. She is stubborn, opinionated and brazen, but she is also extremely generous, thoughtful and soft at her core. She is also the perfect example of how a woman can stand up for herself and overcome the hand that life deals you.

My parents are completely different but are both so strong and compliment each other perfectly in a yin and yang balance. Their marriage, and therefore their home, is filled with love, respect, compromise and so much laughter. It was the best home to grow up in. My mum and dad never restricted me or my brother from doing anything that we wanted. They allowed us room to explore and discover who we wanted to be. They allowed us to make our own mistakes and never dictated to us. Don't get me wrong, there were rules and expectations. We weren't allowed to run riot or disrespect anyone. We were raised to have good manners and morals but raised in a relaxed and unconditionally loving environment. Their marriage is based on a similar foundation of love, respect and unity where they also allow each other space as they understand that it's ok to have different hobbies and interests. In short, they're incredible, and if I hadn't witnessed it continuously over the last 30 years, I don't think I would believe that a relationship like that truly existed.

In the days and weeks that followed David's death, it shocked me how it affected my parents. Obviously, I'm not saying I didn't expect them to grieve, but I had never seen them so vulnerable and so broken and that swept me from my feet. From the second my dad told me, I had to pause however I was feeling. Actually, I couldn't even start any kind of feeling because, like an automatic reaction, I just had to have a clear head and be there for my mum and dad. As I stood in front of my dad, seeing him like that, I felt so helpless and stunned, but a voice in my head just told me to be there for them.

For the first time in my life, I had to be strong for them. I had to support them. I had to think logically, I had to make some decisions and I had to do a lot of running about to make sure they had something in for dinner, clean as much as I could for them, make teas and coffees because people were in and out of their house all day for weeks as well as be there for them emotionally. I'm sure to a lot of people it may have looked like I didn't care. Obviously, that couldn't have been further from the truth. I was dealing with so much stuff but had to push it all down and show a calm exterior for my mum and dad. Don't get me wrong, no one made me feel that way, it was all in my head but they're my mum and dad and I would do it again for them in a heartbeat, but it was definitely not easy. It was never easy. I don't intend it to sound like they were completely unable because they were, I'm also not trying to make it sound as though I am the hero who did it all, because I didn't. All I can tell you is my side of our story and what I felt.

I think that they are both so independent and strong but I also think that's the reason that I found this situation so alien. There were definitely times that they comforted and supported me too, as they always have but when the roles reversed, and I was the one being the caregiver to my parents, it was something that felt so unnatural to me. Obviously, I always loved and cared for them but this was something so far from what I was used to. Imagine trying to make these huge decisions but you still want to be respectful.

I wanted to do everything for them, I wanted to take over so that they didn't have to make difficult decisions, but it was definitely not my place. How the hell was I supposed to know what was the right thing to do? I was experiencing some kind of anti-sibling rivalry. I didn't want to take any attention off David. I wanted to sink into the shadows, quietly cleaning up after everyone, keeping busy, keeping invisible. Keeping helpful so that my mum and dad didn't have to do anything and could just focus on whatever they needed to. In reality, I wanted to fix things. How? I have no idea, it was impossible but when I look back, I realise that's what I was trying to do. I wanted to take their pain away and as much as I knew I couldn't do that, I was trying to do the next best thing to at least soften the edges, even just a little bit. When people would tell me "Your mum and dad say you've been their rock" or "I heard you've been amazing" I just wanted to scream at them. I didn't want their praise. I didn't want their attention. *HELLO? David has just DIED! This is about HIM, not ME! And besides, they're my mum and dad! I'm just doing the only thing for them I can.*

Obviously, I now know that it was meant as a compliment, maybe even a comfort. I also know that people have NO IDEA what to say to someone who is grieving, including myself. I actually found it funny when people would start sympathetic but tried to backtrack on words that had already escaped their mouths. For example, the most common was "*Hi Rhiannon, how are you doing?... well, obviously you're not ok. I can't imagine what you're all going through ....*" The length of the rambling depended on how awkward the person felt. I never took offence to slips of the tongue like this. What started as a well-intentioned greeting, usually left a rambling monologue of them digging an even bigger hole and to me, it was amusing.

Although this is the hardest thing that I've ever had to deal with, and I would much rather it never happened at all, I am grateful that I got to be there for my mum and dad. It will never make up for the millions of amazing things they have done or sacrificed for me and David. But it is nice knowing that I can do something for them, even if the circumstances are anything but nice. Also, as always, they taught me a massive lesson. If Mr. and Mrs. Superhuman (aka mum and dad) have times of difficulty, times of vulnerability and pain, then that means it's ok for the rest of us mere mortals to have moments like that too. In fact, their vulnerability made me respect them so much more (if that was even possible). Their pain came from love. The love they will always share with their son. I admire them more than they will ever know because sometimes, words do not do emotions justice.

It shocked me how quickly I would see my own son comforting me. My eldest, Dane, took my brother's passing the hardest of my three children. Maybe because he is the eldest, maybe because he was so much like David or because they got on so well, who knows? In between trying to be there for my mum and dad, making sure they're ok and not alone, I had to try to be there for Dane too and the pain and confusion he was feeling. How do you explain something like this to a seven-year-old? How can I process this *myself*? We don't even know why he died yet! I couldn't help my children understand his death by saying he was old, or really ill. He was young and as far as we knew, perfectly healthy!

About two months after David died, when things had calmed down with Dane and my mum and dad didn't need me so much, my boys were in bed and Jamie was out, I was in my room trying to meditate and I just broke down and cried uncontrollably. Like a really *ugly* cry. The kind of cry you can only do when you're completely alone and nowhere near a mirror. Like, snot hanging from your face and muscles in your neck flexing, kind of ugly cry. And as I'm writing this, I can hear David saying *"but Ann, That's how you always look"*. Thanks, David.

Anyway, I thought the boys were all sleeping, so I'm not letting go fully with my cry because I don't want to wake them but I'm kind of allowing it to escape as they're all sleeping. Or so I thought, because then in walks Dane with a worried and apprehensive look on his face asking if I'm ok. I was so shocked, but with the state of my face, there is no way I can brush this off and tell him that I'm fine, and part of me doesn't want to. I want him to know that however we feel, it's ok. I've been telling him all this time that it's ok to be happy when you feel happy and it's ok to be sad when you feel sad. So I decide to tell him that I'm just thinking of David and that I'm sad because I miss him, and then smile at him in a way that tells him not to worry. So then, my seven-year-old son walks over and sits next to me on my bed, puts his arms around me and hugs me.

My seven-year-old comforts *me*.

He is being the caregiver here. He is the parent in this moment. He is looking after me and he tells me that he feels sad too and that maybe I should think of some happy times because that makes him feel better. I remember feeling stunned. I was completely shocked and also torn. I was amazed this seven-year-old boy had the emotional ability to be empathetic to his mother, to sympathise with my pain, to be so mature that he would provide a loving and supportive space for me. This kid is literally being my guardian angel right now.

Yet I also felt a massive amount of guilt. He is my baby, he shouldn't have to comfort me. That's not his job. What kind of a mother am I? This, obviously, made me feel worse, yet I couldn't shake the amazement, the admiration and the appreciation I felt towards him. I don't know if he remembers that night or if he will ever know how much of a superhero he was in that moment, but I hope that one day he reads this and will know how proud I am of him. I saw him in a different light that night. I'm in awe thinking about it now.

When I think of what Dane did for me that night, I know that I needed that. I also know that it might have been a good thing that I showed my vulnerability. Like my own parents did for me, I showed Dane that it's ok to not be ok. I accepted and acknowledged my emotions and allowed myself to express them. In that moment, I didn't suppress them and walk around in a bad mood, taking out my own issues on everyone else, like many of us do.

Something I didn't admit to anyone was how bad my anxiety was getting. Jamie was the only person I remember telling and even then, I didn't admit the full extent. My children became my comfort blanket and I didn't want to leave the house. If I had to take them to school, or pop to the shop that was fine as they were with me, but if I had to go by myself, I remember becoming quite shaky and anxious. In fact, I remember one specific time when my sister-in-law had my youngest for the day to give me a break and I left the house to go and collect the other two from school. I physically felt the anxiety surrounding me. I saw the trees and grass vibrating and closing in on me. I kept repeating to myself that it wasn't real, and I focused on breathing deeply. I knew that if I could just get to the school, I would be back with the boys and I would be ok.
Like a small child clinging to the comfort of her parents in the big wide world to feel safe and comforted, I was clinging to my children to keep them close because I needed that security. In this way, they unknowingly became the parent as an automatic response of me reverting back to the child role.

It didn't result in a major problem as it didn't last for too long, but when you've been independent and a free spirit your whole life, the unfamiliarity and restrictiveness of anxiety and agoraphobia can be quite consuming.
I would go back and forth to the school multiple times a day for different clubs the boys had, and that was fine, because at very least I had Casey with me. I

could talk to him and distract myself. But one night, when I was on my own and on my way to an evening class I was attending, I had an anxiety attack and pulled the car over, texted Jamie and told him I don't want to go, and I feel panicky. I remember imagining walking into the class and the anxiety was overpowering. There is no logical explanation for this. I've always felt quite confident within myself and really enjoyed these classes, but after my brother died, it changed me in ways I was unprepared for.

I was freaking out and reached out to Jamie as he is also my comfort blanket and I just wanted him to tell me to come home and it will all be ok so that I would feel justified to give in to this emotion. But he didn't. He told me that he hates that I'm going through this but if that's how I feel, I need to keep going and just do it or I will always allow myself to turn back when I feel that anxiety creeping in and it'll get worse and worse.

I remember looking at my phone in shock. This was the last thing that I wanted to hear and the last thing I expected him to say, but it was absolutely the thing that I *needed* to hear. It was tough, I didn't like it but he was right and it definitely contributed to me feeling more confident and independent again and not needing to lean on my children in order to feel protected and comforted. *Damn you, Jamie!*

At times of intense emotion such as grief, it seems the hierarchy of family roles goes out the window. Where there is love and compassion there cannot be a hierarchy. You want to help and support everyone you love no matter if that's your child, parent, grandparent or anyone else. It's important we allow this love and support and not block it. In times of weakness, we receive strength from sources we may not have anticipated but as it is intended as a gift that wants to be given, it's important that we accept it with gratitude. Pride has to take a back seat as it has no place when true love is being shared. Who in your life willingly wants to love and support you? Perhaps you may have unconsciously been rejecting their gift?

<u>Chapter 4</u>
Feeling alone in a crowd of familiar faces

"You don't have to see the whole staircase. Just take the first step"
-Martin Luther King

Following David's death, my mum and dad's house was always full of people. Family and friends who lived near and far came to offer their condolences, love and services. They came to pay their respects to both David and to us. I remember seeing so much love pouring into their home every day. It really was beautiful to see that so many people cared so deeply. It was almost as if my mum and dad were enveloped in a cocoon of love, thoughts and prayers.

I know that it was directed at me too, and I was grateful, I still am, but I'm also grateful that when I went home, there was no one there except Jamie and the boys. I, like my brother, like having my own space. I love being around my friends and family too, but I need balance, too much of one or the other throws me off. Being at my mum's house, with different people constantly coming and going while having to repeat the same conversations, answer the same questions time and time again was really draining for me. I know that people were just trying to help and wanted to know how we were doing, if we'd heard anything from the coroner and if there was anything they could do, which is why I smiled and answered questions, especially if it meant my mum and dad didn't have to keep doing it, but I was glad to go home to my safe and quiet place with my comfort blanket of my husband and children.

It didn't matter how many people were in the room, I always felt alone. I always wanted to shrink into the shadows. Sometimes I did this by being quiet, sometimes I busied myself by making teas and coffees, sometimes I joined in conversations just to be 'part of the crowd' and to not draw attention to my true feelings but in reality, I was just doing what I needed to do to get through each day, hour or minute. I was going through the motions of the day but inside I was screaming. I wanted to open up and let the monster out, but I felt like I couldn't because I knew no one could resonate with my pain.

I found that if I started to open up about how I feel, people would sympathise and go on to give their own experiences and emotions. I was grateful that I had many people that I could open up to, but it didn't help me because I never did. I started to get bitter and angry. Yes, we were all grieving for the same person but no one else had lost their brother. No one else knew what it was like to lose their brother, David.

Everyone, and I mean *everyone*, had someone to grieve with or alongside. I felt that everyone had someone who could understand and sympathise with their pain. My mum and dad both lost their son, my sons all lost their uncle, my nan and grandad both lost their grandson, my aunties all lost their nephew, our cousins all lost their cousin and a large group of people lost a great friend.

I felt like everyone had someone to stand next to them while they walked this dark and grief-ridden path. Yet I stood alone. I walked alone. I had no one to match my relationship. The one person that could have done that was the same person we were grieving. No one else had our inside jokes or childhood memories to share and no one else had to listen to their mum and dad arrange their son's funeral and start making arrangements for their own when they were picking out a plot for David. Which then lead me to realise that not only am I walking this alone, there will come a day when I have to walk that path alone too. When the day finally comes for them to reunite with David, my brother will not be here for me to walk alongside while I mourn my parents. It doesn't really matter how amazing or supportive Jamie or anyone else is, this is not something anyone else can understand because David was only *my* brother. This is something that, now, I take great pride in. Although it was difficult and lonely in the beginning, now, I am proud and kind of glad that no one else knows what it was like to have David as a brother. It makes me feel special and I know that it is something that I have all to myself.

For a long time, no one knew the full extent of how I felt. It's only now, well over a year later, and a hell of a lot of soul-searching that I understand why. I was scared. Scared and also I felt kind of repressed.

I thought that if I was honest about how I felt, that I wouldn't be able to stop crying and that if people saw me crying, it would be greeted with "*Don't cry, I know it's difficult, I miss him too*". I always took this comment as really dismissive. Dismissive of my feelings and the very sudden, traumatic and heartbreaking loss of my brother. In truth, I just wanted to be heard. Uninterrupted, unapologetic and raw. I wanted to be allowed the opportunity and the space to fully express how I felt without someone trying to make me feel better in any way.

The worst part is, I know I've said something along these lines too because the truth is, it comes from a place of love. It's not intended as dismissive or repressing, it's intended as a form of comfort and encouragement. As much as I know this now, I wish someone had told me this at the time. I wish someone had told me that it's ok to cry. We all have individual relationships and no two are the same.

It got to the point when I didn't and wouldn't talk to anyone about my feelings. Now and again when things bubbled too high inside me, I would break down to Jamie. He knew that I didn't want to necessarily talk, I just needed to release. I wanted him to hold me so I felt comforted and supported. He knew that nothing he could say or anything I could hear would miraculously change my emotional state. I just needed love. I think we all need to be more like this. Just offer love. You don't have to know the right thing to say or offer your own wisdom. Just offer love and support.

I don't blame any of my family or friends for 'making' me feel dismissed because they didn't intentionally do it. They were just offering love and support and trying to cheer me up. They were doing the best they could the best way they knew how, and besides, we all know this was way more about what I was doing wrong than what they were doing.

We are all so different and grief (as well as happiness) is different for all of us. We are the only ones who can alter our states. We can't expect someone to read our mind and know what will best for us because most of the time, we don't even know what it is ourselves.

I realised that I was isolating myself because '*no one understood my pain*'. I singled myself out and labelled myself as a victim. How self-righteous, right?
We were all suffering. No two relationships are the same, but because I was the only one who could label David as my biological brother, I felt even more alone. I'm not beating myself up about it, though. I was hurt and had no idea how to deal with the agony I was in. I'm just grateful that I'm not still in that headspace and can see things a little clearer now.

After a few months, my emotions were becoming too much for me to handle alone, and although I had plenty of offers to 'have a chat whenever I need it', I still couldn't tell anyone exactly how I felt. Not the full extent anyway. I had told different people snippets, but no single person knew everything. I had found a few ways that helped me cope on a day-to-day basis, but I also knew I needed more.

Sometimes I got really angry with myself. I desperately wanted to speak out and ask for help or at least a friendly ear to listen to me. It's not like I didn't have offers, but there's something inside me that wouldn't allow it. Something would always hold me back. I knew I had to do something, and if I'm honest, I knew that I had to speak about what and how I felt. I don't do well feeling vulnerable, but it felt like a raging scream was growing inside me, increasing the pressure and was only a matter of time before steam and whistling escaped from my ears.

My dad had spoken up and went to see a bereavement counsellor. I was, and still am, so proud of him. He spoke up. To admit you need help is such a strong and brave thing to do. It's something so easy in theory, yet it comes so unnaturally to us. No one can do or cope with everything, yet we seem to think we should have all the answers. We don't.

After a few weeks, I decided that I was going to finally speak up too. If I can admire and praise my dad for speaking up, I should do it too. It wasn't easy, though. It went against my stubborn nature, but I felt like it was the best option for me at that time. Generally, I found talking to a stranger an easier idea to cope with and I hoped that he or she would be able to offer some type of advice or coping mechanisms or at the very least, tell me what I was feeling was normal.

When I made my initial appointment, I committed to going into this full throttle. If I was going to do this, I was going to do it properly. No holding back, no prettying up my words or saying what I *thought* was the right thing to say. It was time to be completely honest, no matter how brutal or raw it was.

I was terrified and way outside of my comfort zone, but I did think that it would help me, especially after going for a few sessions. I knew that talking to a stranger would be easier for me as I didn't need to withhold an image and therefore feel freer to express myself. Well, low and behold, I was wrong. You'd have thought that I would have realised by now that maybe I don't have all the answers.

The woman who counselled me was really lovely and did actually suggest some things that were helpful, but I found there was no life or animation in our conversation. By this, I mean that she would suggest or point out things that for most people would have made sense, but were completely wrong for my circumstances, for my family. We're not your *typical* family and I'm proud of that, but when someone tries to offer scenarios that do not fit with you, it's hard to allow a conversation to flow as I had to keep explaining things or personalities. Basically, it was made very clear to me that this woman was a complete stranger and that I was sharing my most sacred and deepest emotions with her. I'm so glad that I went to that counselling session as it gave me the realisation (and kick up the bum) I needed to speak out. I didn't want to sit here with a stranger, I realised. I wanted to talk to my husband and to my mum and dad. People, who know exactly who we all are, know what David is like, know our circumstances and quirks, know our relationships and personalities.

Sometimes it may be easier for you to talk to a stranger. It seemed to really help my dad, and I thought this would be the case for me too, but I was wrong. It just reinforced that you shouldn't presume you know what will work and what won't. You don't necessarily know what is best for you, or how you'll react in these types of circumstances. Having an open mind is so important and sometimes trial and error is the only way forward. You have to give things a go and be prepared to drop them when they are not helping you move forward.

If I had convinced myself that "this is who I am. I find it easier to talk to someone on the outside", then I would have wasted a lot of time, energy and patience. Instead, I listened to my gut instincts and knew that this wasn't helping me. It didn't feel right. I knew the people that I needed to speak to and I wanted to do it at a time that felt natural when emotions arose and not on a scheduled time and date.

To many, it may have seemed like a failure, as just another thing that wasn't helping, but I saw this as a massive success. I had been holding back for months because '*I found it easier to talk to someone on the outside*' and so I wasn't allowing myself to open up and release the emotions properly. Yet, as soon as I actually spoke to someone on the outside, I realised that this wasn't what I wanted. The people I wanted to speak to were next to me all along.

I didn't come to this realisation and miraculously become this really open person who shares exactly how they feel, unfortunately, I'm still a stubborn old mule, but I am trying to be open. I'm trying to share how I feel instead of trapping it inside and let it bubble, instead of trying to *deal* with it all by myself, which actually translates to 'trying my hardest to ignore and suppress it, so really, *not* dealing with it'.

We all know that every human on this planet is individual. We can have similarities in our mannerisms, interests and even looks, but no two people are exactly the same. This is why no two relationships are the same. We all have a unique bond to the people in our lives and unique memories. Grief affects us all differently and I mean this in two ways.

Grieving the loss of David, affected all my family differently because we're all different people with different personalities therefore, we all grieved differently for David. But if I had another brother who also died, I, as one individual would grieve differently for each of them because, although they would both be my brothers, I would have individual relationships with each of them. Therefore... Grief is a bitch. It's not a one-size-fits-all deal. Don't presume you know what to do or how to deal with things because you've grieved in the past.

We're also constantly changing and evolving as human beings. Our interests and beliefs shift over time and you must keep an open mind to what may or may not work to give you more peace and a more joyous life because no matter how much you grieve or how strong your pain is, you do deserve a peaceful and joyous life.

Finding an outlet where you can channel or at least acknowledge your emotions is so important. Grief is not just about crying and feeling sad as I have said before. Find a healthy way for you to deal with whatever you need to while working towards an amazing life, because life is way too short to be holding yourself back. What have you always wanted to do or achieve that you can start working toward now?

Chapter 5
Numbing the pain

"If you're always trying to be normal you will never know how amazing you can be."
-Maya Angelou

Humans are very emotional beings. It's natural for a human to experience many different emotions throughout the day, it's almost like a rollercoaster in that our emotions are up one minute, down the next. Life is a constant shift in emotions as we react to our internal and external environments.

All emotions are temporary, however we have got into a bad habit of using our language in a way that implies we *are* our emotions. We say things like "I'm depressed", "I'm a happy person" and "I have anxiety". In reality, we just *feel* these things. We *feel* depressed, we *feel* happy and we *feel* anxious. It's a temporary emotion, which can change at any point. You can definitely have emotions that you tend to feel more than others, but I believe that it's important to understand that experiencing a range of emotions is healthy.

For example, let's say that you're usually a happy person. You're quite optimistic; you are generally positive and like to look on the bright side of life and to feel good. That's great. But it's also ok to feel sadness if someone you love is hurt. It's ok to feel anxious if you're about to take a massive step towards a big goal you have. It's ok to feel guilty that you forgot your son had swimming and so didn't send him to school with his swimming stuff.

Our emotions are there to tell us something or to help us learn. If you feel happy, you are aware of the things that lift your spirits. If you feel anxious, you know you are uncertain about a particular outcome and very possibly out of your comfort zone (although this shouldn't automatically be taken as a negative. A lot of the time, it's times like this that help us grow into better and more abundant versions of ourselves). Similarly, if you believe that you're an anxious person, ask yourself if you're anxious 24/7? It might feel like that at times. But are you anxious when you brush your teeth? Are you anxious about how to put your socks on? Are you anxious about your name? The names of your friends and family?

If we hear something enough times, we will begin to believe it. If all your life, you've told yourself that you're stupid and can never get anything right, the chances are you'll have very little confidence and will have a whole list of 'failures' that you've achieved. On the other hand, if you've always told yourself that you're a superstar and can achieve anything you put your mind to, chances are you're winning at life and very possibly don't even recognise your 'failures' and just saw them as hurdles or course-correction on the way to your goals.
What you tell yourself will manifest into your reality because you believe it to be true.

Although it's natural to experience the spectrum of emotions, it's also natural to lean towards emotions that light you up and make you feel safe and lean away from emotions that bring discomfort and uncertainty. However, some people can find comfort and feel safe in emotions that do not serve them fully. For example, if your story is that you're anxious or depressed, it can act as a form of your identity and you may cling to those traits as a comfort blanket because it's familiar for you to behave that way. During grief, we do this a lot. We allow the sticky web of grief to hold us up and support us. It's complex and we don't understand it fully, we're already tangled in it, so it's easy to give in and just hang there because we are dealing with so much that we may not know what else to do. So, we chose to *become* grief, perhaps even unconsciously. We allow it to become a part of our identity and therefore carry it around with us always. Sometimes, we convince ourselves that if we're not grieving, then we mustn't love the person, so you cling to the grief. I know I did this. It took a while for me to realise that my love for my brother is a much stronger emotion than my grieving for him. When you're experiencing grief, it's a very uncertain and uncomfortable time. You may never have experienced such conflicting emotions and you can find yourself scared and not knowing how to cope on numerous occasions. It can be a stressful time and there are definitely times where I wanted to cave in and throw myself down on the floor to slide down the slippery slope. It would have been a lot easier in the beginning, but not in the long run.

I never had a plan. I never set out to become a '*better*' person but I'm trying my hardest. I have slipped up plenty of times. I still do. Isn't that what being human is all about? It's not a mistake if you learn from it, it's a lesson. Sometimes when I really didn't know what to do or how to cope, I considered drinking away my sorrows or taking drugs to numb the pain. It's not my proudest thought, I'll admit, but I am proud that I didn't do it. I mean, I couldn't. I'm a very visual person and yes, my mind works overtime to create extreme images. It doesn't do things by halves. When I considered drinking away my sorrows, my mind pulled up an image of me lying face down in a gutter with the police finding me and having to call my husband. When I considered taking drugs to numb the pain, my mind pulled up a very vivid image of me in a hospital bed with my mum and dad standing at my side, in tears, mourning not just the death of their son, but now watching their daughter ruin her life in a downward spiral.

How could I do that to my family? My husband was holding things together at home; he didn't deserve to deal with that too. My kids didn't really understand why their 30-year-old uncle died in his sleep and they had to watch their mum's family distraught and wracked with grief, they deserved better from me. Not to mention that my mum and dad were going through something that no parent should have to go through, let alone they are two of the most loving, funny, good, kind and generous parents that have ever blessed this earth. How dare I add to their stress and pain. How dare I waste my life when my brothers' was cut way too short? It was in that moment that I realised that not only was it ok for me to live my life, but I kind of had to live a bigger and better life because now I was doing it for me and for him.

I decided that I would only do things that made me feel good. Not what other people thought I should do or what everyone else was doing. I was going to be really honest with myself and ask what feels right. Not just for an instant hit, but in my gut, what feels right and will bring me the most joy. Sometimes that meant reflecting or having a good cry. Sometimes I wanted to watch home videos of us, even though I knew it would result in tears, it would also bring love into my heart. There were also times where I wanted to be completely selfish and do something solely for me and not think about anything or anyone else.

I also made a point of telling myself not to bite off more than I could chew, to take things slowly and just focus on now. Then I made a point of allowing myself mistakes. By this, I don't mean to make a stupid decision that I knew I would regret later but justify it by allowing myself some 'slip-ups'. I mean that if I looked back and realised it was a mistake, to forgive it, recognise it and learn from it. For example, if I took my anger and frustration out on someone and later realised they didn't deserve that, then I could recognise it as a mistake, learn from it and I would apologize.

What we have to realise is that nothing we can say or do can turn back time, as much as we'd like it to. But what you say and do 100% has an effect on the present and the future. Therefore, going off the rails will not bring back your loved one any more than knitting a scarf will, but the difference is one is a 'quick fix' that ends up being a longer fix because you're not acknowledging your emotions so they're just going to keep coming back until they're heard *and* now you have to nurse a hangover and/or a come down... then the other is considered to be therapeutic *and* will keep your neck warm in the winter.

It's about finding something that works for you. If knitting isn't your thing, try woodwork, going for a walk, volunteering, sign up for a course you've always wanted to do, learn a new language, learn to play an instrument, read, write, join local coffee morning groups, find a new TV series to watch. Find what works for you, but also realise that you will want to switch things up.

Let's take a random day for example. When you wake up you might want to watch your new TV show.

After a few episodes, you might get bored and decide you want to have a shower then do your hair and put some makeup on.

After that, you could feel like taking a walk, and as you fancy something sweet, think to yourself, *"why not walk to the local bakery to get a cake*? "

You get home and fancy a cup of tea with your cake. You could carry on watching your TV show, but no, you think you want to phone your best friend for a catch-up, he always makes you laugh and puts you in a good mood.

Your friend helped you to realise that you want to reach out to some people who may be experiencing similar things to you, so you go online and search for charities or organisations that may run groups local to you.

Later that night, you remember that documentary that you recorded about polar bears and you decide that you want to watch it.

This is not about obsessing over something or thinking too far ahead. It's about doing what works in the now. You wouldn't want to do only one thing for the rest of your life. You have to switch things up, so things don't stagnate and become mundane.

Sometimes you will want to be around people, other times you may want to be by yourself. Sometimes you will want to eat junk food, other times you might fancy a salad. It's fine to want different things at different times. Listen to your intuition and follow it to what is going to make you content in that moment. I once heard a quote by Lao Tzu, an ancient Chinese philosopher, which really stuck with me.

"If you are depressed you are living in the past. If you are anxious you are living in the future. If you are at peace you are living in the present."

This does not mean to ignore everything that has ever happened to you or to be in denial about anything. I believe we all feel sad or depressed at times, just as we all feel anxious too. However, this doesn't mean you have to remain in those states. Try not to dwell too much on one emotion.

When I decided that I was not going to self-destruct and try to live a full life, I needed to find some positive ways to either deal with what I was going through or at least something that wouldn't tip me over the edge. My brother's death was a major shock to us all and I had never lost anyone so close or so unexpectedly, so I was completely clueless as to how to deal with this trauma. I decided that I would be open to suggestions. That I would give anything a go if it sounded like it might work for me. In reality, I had no idea what worked for me, as I'd never been here before.
Over time, I have found a few different ways that helped me cope a bit better. My hope is that you will read them and it will inspire a thought or suggestion

you could try, although I must stress again, that everyone is different and what worked for me may not work for you. So be open and give things a go as you could be surprised.

In the very early days, I would go to my mum and dad's house. I would clean, make teas, answer the door and generally made myself busy so that I could occupy my mind. To be completely honest, I was scared of stopping. If I was no longer busy, I thought it would hit me like a ton of bricks. It did… eventually, but initially, I knew my focus had to be on my mum and dad. Doing whatever I could for them had to be my main priority. Since then, however, I have slowed down a lot. I allow my feeling and emotions to come and I definitely allow them to go. I take time out for myself; I'm kinder to myself and allow myself the time and space to heal.

Even though I have slowed down massively, cleaning seems to be a habit that has stayed. I don't think my house has ever been so tidy! I'm not complaining mind you, I can think of worse habits to have. I'm not obsessive with it, but I have got into an effective routine and enjoy being in a clean and tidy environment. I find it quite therapeutic to clean and look after my space, it allows me to relax more in a more pleasant environment and there is lots of evidence that proves that decluttering your home and/or work environment helps you to declutter your mind. I can definitely say it has worked for me. Again, don't think too big or too dramatically. If your house is in desperate need of some attention, focus on one room right now, and in that room, focus on one section. Are there loads of papers on your dining table? Does the TV stand need dusting? Is there a big pile of washing up in the sink?

You'll be surprised at how satisfying it is to see the transformations you are creating and will soon get the bug for it. When you walk into a room, you want to think "*ahhhh*" deep breath out and shoulders relaxing and not "**ERGH**" screwing your nose up and turning your head the other way in disgust, to add to your list of reasons to feel crappy.

The key here is lots of little wins that lead to one giant one. Cleaning is said to have many benefits on improving your mood, your health (both mental and physical), your family, your confidence and your motivation. I mean, you could just hire a cleaner, and that's fine. Life is too short to be forced into things you really hate. But unless you're going to hire a full-time in-house cleaner to tidy everything 24/7, then you need to get friendly with the day-to-day cleaning habits that will improve your day-to-day mood. Cleaning down the kitchen surfaces, decluttering that pile of letters (as well as taking your head out of the sand with bills and sorting them out), taking out cups and mugs when you go into the kitchen.

Get everyone on board. If you live with other people, make sure that communal areas have a rota or schedule and make sure everyone is pulling their weight. Make sure kids bring down cups from their bedrooms and they tidy up their toys before they go bed. If everyone takes responsibility for their own stuff, life will run a lot more smoothly.

I know cleaning isn't for everyone. I know that it's generally looked as an unwanted chore that never ends (*trust me, I have three kids!*), and you can put things off up to a point, but sooner or later, you're going to have to wash some clothes around here or scrub a plate or two if you don't want to eat your dinner off a paper plate. If you can learn to put on your favourite songs and take it as time for yourself, knowing that at the end of it, you're going to make a nice cup of coffee and sit in silence sighing with relief at your beautifully clean and tidy home until you have to pick your children up from school, it's amazing!… Or is that just me? Trust me; it's the simple things in life that bring the most pleasure.

Something that always puts me in a good mood, is cooking. It's not necessarily that I love to cook, but more that I love to eat. My family are big foodies and we love to catch up with good food. Anyone who knows me will know I love my food and I soon realised that unless I won the lottery and could eat out every night, I would have to learn to cook some go-to dishes if I wanted to eat proper hearty meals. I mean, I don't mind chicken nuggets and fish fingers now and again, but I don't want to have them all the time. To me, cooking is just a necessary part of how I get to eat the food, like buying the ingredients.

I'm more savoury than sweet so I tend to try out new recipes for main courses than baking. Although, not to brag, but my homemade banana and chocolate chip cake, still warm from the oven, puts me in a good mood just thinking about it.

Cooking has been made into this belief that it's very difficult and precise and takes so long and is expensive. I call B.S. on this. I have had to learn (or invent) lots of dinners that don't cost a lot of money and I have found so many more that don't include standing in a kitchen for hours on end, *because... who has the time for that every night?*

I don't really use them too often, but slow cookers are a great invention for this. You throw everything in, turn it on and later that evening, you have a great meal with very little effort involved. Try it all out and see what works for you. Ask someone you know who is good at cooking or has a large family (therefore, little time).

I'm not preaching about eating more veggies (although, as a nation, we definitely do need to up our veg intake), I'm just saying eat a variety of things that feel good. That could mean making a curry that you have seen on a program or a hearty dinner that your mum used to cook. One of my children's' favourite things to do during the school holidays, is to look through some recipe books they won at a school fair, and find a recipe they want to make. Of course, it's usually the chocolatiest and sugar-packed recipe they can find, but that's ok. It's a treat and doesn't happen every day. It's a fun activity for us to enjoy together and we get to eat something delicious at the end.

I'm well aware that I have just suggested cooking and cleaning as a way to lift your spirits, and I must be painting myself into an image of a domestic goddess, or a sexist stereotype from the 1950s. Please do not be fooled. I can think of many things I would rather be doing than cooking or cleaning, and I definitely don't want to do either for too long each day, but I also know when I'm feeling down, sometimes I have to go back to basics and build myself up from the inside out. I focus on my mental health and wellbeing and what I put into my body to help my mood improve. I do not, however, do all the cooking and cleaning in my household. My husband is a great cook and really puts a lot of time and effort into his dishes and he also helps a lot with our kids and household stuff too when he's not at work. My children (all boys) are expected to pull their weight too. It's the little things like taking their plates out to the kitchen after they have finished their meal or wiping down the sink after they have brushed their teeth. If they are asked to do a 'job', they are expected to do it, and they always do. In our home, we all rise to the occasion.

My point is, that sometimes, in order to feel better, it's a lot deeper and a lot more basic than a night out or a trip to a theme park (and probably cheaper too).

Another thing that really helped me was physical exercise. I'm not a fan of going to the gym and spending a few hours doing something you hate because it's what society tells us we 'should' do. Our bodies do need to move, stretch and receive some oxygen, though. My favourite ways to do this are yoga, running or going for a walk, depending on what mood I am in. Sometimes I really need to release a burst of energy, clear my head and feel air pour into my lungs. This is when running is good for me. Other times, I will feel tight and tense and off balance and I need to stretch my body, reconnect and enjoy some yoga. Sometimes, I just feel like going for a stroll, taking in the sights where I live and appreciating my environment, so I talk a walk around my local park or to the shops instead of driving.

Yoga has been especially beneficial to me during my difficult times. It has helped me to reconnect to my body and to my breath, to really take notice and appreciate how my body moves and just how incredible the human body is. It's amazing to me, that something as simple as breathing is something we massively take for granted. So, when you become aware of your breathing and tap into just how powerful you really are, it really helps to put a lot into perspective.

There have been many studies on the benefits of exercise and the links to improved mental health when people increase their exercise. It's a vicious circle of feeling bad (e.g. grief), so eating badly (e.g. comfort eating), not moving your body (lying in bed all day) and feeding your brain lots of negative self-talk (e.g. "Why me?", "I can't do anything right" or "Life is so unfair"). It feels so difficult to get out of it. Surely, to feel better doesn't just include going for a walk? Well... no, it doesn't. But it will help. Going for a walk and getting some fresh air in your lungs will help towards a better and brighter day. If you want to join a kickboxing class to help you channel your emotions in a positive way, I think that's great.
As I said before, suppressing your emotions will not fast-track anything. You need to find a way to healthily channel your anger, confusion, sadness or whatever you may be feeling at the time, and exercise is a great way to help to release but also gain some clarity or headspace that could be really beneficial.

If you really want to get out of a rut, you need to become aware of your internal dialogue. Years ago, it was believed that talking to yourself was the first sign of insanity. Now, we know that that's not quite true. We all talk to ourselves. ALL. THE. TIME. Have you ever been giving yourself a pep talk and recited the words *"come on, you can do this!"*?

Or made a mistake and heard a snarling voice in your head saying *"Well done, genius. Messed up again! Why are you such an idiot?!"?*

Have you tried to walk in high heels and repeated *"Don't trip. Don't trip. Don't trip"?*

We all talk to ourselves and it's this little voice that we overlook that actually determines most of the things that we allow to happen to us in life. It dictates if we believe we are worthy of going for something or if we're 'not good enough'.

I could go on for ages here, but that's a whole other book by its self. The main point is to become aware of what you're telling yourself. If you're telling yourself "I'm sad" all the time, chances are that's how you will continue to feel because our internal state affects our external state. If you tell yourself "I'm *feeling* sad at this point in time, but that's ok. I miss my brother and my sadness is just an extension of the love I have for him" It really changes the depth of the emotion.

I'm not saying you have to lie to yourself (although sometimes it can definitely feel like that), but it's time to really add some technicolour to our black and white perceptions on emotions, life and of the world. We used to believe that confidence was something you were born with. Either you had it or you didn't. We're lucky enough to live in an age where this was proved to be incorrect. Confidence is a by-product of positive and encouraging self-talk.

I want you to become really aware of what you're saying to yourself and even correct yourself. *"No, I'm not an idiot. Although I may mess up sometimes, I also get a lot of things right and some things I even get right on my first try. Practice makes perfect and I'm one step closer."* Let's not forget that Thomas

Edison 'failed' over 9,000 times before he successfully invented the light bulb. Thank god his internal dialogue said "ok, so that's another way we know that will **not** work. I can do this!"

The way we talk to ourselves determines so many aspects of our lives and we need to, firstly, become aware of it and, secondly, learn to take control of the words and tone in which we speak to ourselves in. If you don't believe me, try it for a day. Become aware of your internal dialogue and speak to yourself in a negative tone. Use the bullying and nasty words we regularly tell ourselves then see how you feel at the end of the day. You will notice bad or unlucky things happening repeatedly, you'll feel really down within yourself, you may notice your physical appearance change, or you don't 'look your best', you may find yourself in toxic or unpleasant situations with colleagues, friends or family.

Then the next day, remaining aware of your internal dialogue, wake up telling yourself "today is going to be a great day!" Compliment yourself in the mirror; check out your sexy self. On the day you compliment yourself and give yourself encouragement and support, you will find the day brings so many little joys and opportunities, you will *feel* luckier and doors will open for you.

Your internal state affects how you carry yourself externally, you then unconsciously send out signals to your environment and attract things to you with a similar frequency. This is why when you stub your toe as soon as you wake up in the morning, you can get into a bad mood and then you notice your day gets worse and worse. Be aware and keep it positive.

The next thing that really helped me is always a bit of a touchy subject to a lot of people. There are so many stereotypes and judgements placed around it. I guess that we humans do that when we don't fully understand something. We belittle, shame and make up stories as to why it's 'wrong'. For some reason, we decide it's better to put down something that we don't do ourselves rather than just accept that we're all different and everyone is entitled to have their own likes and beliefs.

I talk about meditation more deeply in this book, so I won't bang on about it. But if you're open to suggestions, give it a go. It really helped me. It helped me massively through my bad times and continues to help me through my good times and on a day-to-day basis. During my bad days, meditation helps me to understand and process my emotions, without being all consumed by them and allowing them to take over causing me to react then regret then rectify. During my good days, meditation allows me to witness all my blessings and intensifies the good feelings. It raises my energy even further and I take the time to appreciate whatever wonderful things that I am experiencing that day. On a day to day basis, meditation really helps me to process life, it allows me to take a break and just check in with myself how I am feeling and what's happening with my mind and body.

Recently, my uncle told me about his new hobby of fishing and all the new equipment that he has bought with his birthday money. As he was talking, I noticed how happy and passionate he was. Although I have zero interest in fishing, I was so delighted to carry on this conversation because I could see how happy it made him by talking about it. I was asking him questions and encouraging him to tell me more. He explained that he enjoyed the peace and quiet while fishing and he was left alone with his thoughts in the fresh air and time to process life in general.

By taking the time to let him explain his hobby, even though I have never experienced it, nor did I have any intention to, I found that his reasons, and end result, were very similar to mine for practicing meditation. Not to mention, he lit up when he was given permission to express and tell of his joy, which in turn, made my soul light up, and the world definitely needs more of that.

We need to allow people to be exactly who they are without the fear of being shamed or rejected.

As stated before, writing has been an absolutely amazing tool for me during this process. In the past, I stumbled across writing as a form of release. It was never a daily habit for me to write a journal but more a one-off exercise that I found helped me process how I was feeling. Yet I found that it not only helped me to be able to put things into perspective that may be clouded behind emotion, but I was able to solve questions, the answers to which I thought I didn't know.

After deciding that I was going to try to find productive ways to channel and make sense of my grief, writing popped up in my mind. It had worked before, so I gave it a go, and as I hoped it would, it became such a helpful tool to offload the weight I was carrying. It allowed me to shine a bit of light in such a dark and terrifying time.

Sometimes I would cry as I was releasing all the emotions that had built up inside me. Sometimes I would write happy memories with my brother or a letter to him, saying all the things I am wishing I could say out loud, or that I wished I had said to his face. Sometimes I would write about my day, with my children, husband or parents, things I am grateful for or even things I planned to do in the future. Basically, I wrote about anything and everything.

Writing became my go-to form of coping. I knew it was a space where I could express exactly how I was feeling with no chance of interruption, judgement, pity, questioning or reminding people of the pain they were feeling too. When I would write, there was no one to say, "It will get easier with time" or "He wouldn't want you to cry". I'm as stubborn as they come and need to do things my way and what worked for me, and this seemed to be it.

I remember taking my notebook with me everywhere. I needed to have it close to me in case I needed to pour my emotions into it. I needed to know it was near, so I had a way to grieve. For some reason, talking to someone wasn't an option and only really happened when my emotions built so high that they erupted from the inside out.

I would put my notebook and pens in my handbag when I went to my mum and dad's house, to my mother-in-law's or even just to the shop. I had it near me during the day at home and took it to bed with me at night so it was at hand whenever I needed it. Most of the time when I was out, I wouldn't even use my notebook but just knowing that I had it near was a huge comfort to me.

I'm happy to report that the urgency has subsided now, and I don't need to be within three feet of my notebook anymore, but it is a habit that I have continued ever since. I still journal and write my feelings, but now, instead of a couple of times a day, I journal a couple of times a week. I still like to take it with me if I'm going out for a long period of time, but it's to either use as a notebook, for lists or things I need to remember, or if I'm having a down day where I feel a bit fragile and think I might need to vent. The things I write about, vary depending on how I'm feeling. Similar to meditation, when I'm down, my writing becomes a way for me to gain clarity but also vent and release. Then, when I'm happy, writing becomes a way to reinforce and celebrate all the amazing things that have happened that day, or in my life in general.

Sometimes I just want to vent without burdening anyone, other times I write my dreams, goals and desires and even put them into plans, so they would come to fruition. I can do all of this in the comfort and safety of my own bubble without fear of anyone popping it, either intentionally or unintentionally. I didn't have to worry about my handwriting, how I looked, if the other person understood what I was saying or how it was intended or even hurting anyone's feelings. I could write freely and know that the words and emotions were leaving my head and getting off my chest, off my shoulders and cascading onto the paper, freeing me and leaving me lighter and unburdened. Never underestimate a pen, some paper and the power you have within yourself to work magic.

I found different things helped me at different times and different things that I wouldn't have suspected that actually worked for me. All we want is for someone to tell us what will work and how we feel *normal* again. But why feel *normal* when you can feel *amazing*? Let's take things at baby-steps here and just focus on feeling freer. Grieving means carrying a whole lot of weight on your shoulders so let's focus on releasing that. Be open and explore what may work for you. You may, like me, be surprised, so don't rule anything out. Can you think of some things that could help you now?

Chapter 6
The last time I saw him

"When you speak, you're repeating information you already know, but if you listen, you might learn something new."

-Dalai Lama

Three days before he died, David babysat for me so that I could go to an interview. It was the first and last time I ever left one of my children in his care. Not because I didn't trust him, but because he lived away during the early years that I was raising my children. I used to take my eldest two to visit him during the school holidays as he lived near the beach.

On the Tuesday before he died David looked after Casey for me and I feel torn about this. I feel grateful that he did that for me and that he got to spend some time with his nephew, who he loved; but I also feel bad because he had a bit of a cold and didn't tell me as he knew that I would have cancelled my interview so he didn't have to look after Casey (I didn't get the job anyway).

David was an extremely generous person. I know people always praise lost loved ones but in this case, it's true. Don't get me wrong, I'm honest about David, I love him dearly and have so many fond memories with him, but let's not be deluded. He was the messiest person I have ever met, he was sarcastic and insulting and so annoying. Yet, somehow, he never came across malicious or horrible. That was just him. He was funny with it. He had a gift of insulting us all then sitting there as if butter wouldn't melt and you couldn't help but laugh. His awful impressions of us were my favourite. The fact that they sounded nothing like any of us, took the insult away and just left the humour.

But the day of my interview was not the last time I saw him. Following his death, I literally saw him everywhere. In the supermarket, in the street, at the school, at the park. Obviously, it wasn't actually him, but I saw him in all these people. I never realised how many people looked like David. How many people were as tall as him. How many people had his hair and walked identically to him. So many times I had to do a double-take to make sure it wasn't him.

For a long time, it felt as if he would walk through the front door, oblivious to everything that was going on, living in his own bubble as always and look up confused asking "What's happened here, is everything ok?"

I remember having to tell people that he had died. His work, his best friends. I felt like I was lying. Like I was playing some kind of sick joke on people. It felt like a lie every time I said it out loud. Maybe that's why I kept seeing him. By the way, I wasn't deluded. I was with him on two separate occasions after he left his body. Once on the night he died and once in the funeral home. This is another example of how grief affects you. I had always thought cemeteries to be morbid and then the thought of seeing a dead body freaks me out. But he was my big brother. There was no way this wasn't happening but still, I saw him everywhere.

In my worst days, when I was feeling.... empty? It's very hard to describe what I felt. Sometimes I didn't really feel anything. Just a kind of nothingness. As if I was in autopilot mode, taking care of kids and not seeing, hearing or feeling anything. Like a robot. When I felt like this, I liked to go to the cemetery where David is laid to rest. I like to go alone, no children to be strong for and no adults so that I could ugly cry all I wanted to.

What surprised me was how peaceful I found it. It also opened my eyes to losing loved ones. As I looked around, I saw so many bright and beautiful fresh flowers, balloons, cards and toys. I saw people come and go to lay flowers or just pay their respects to their loved ones. It made me realise that although we have lost someone, we haven't lost the love, the bond. That's why I was sitting there. That's why the man and lady to my right got out the car with a bunch of flowers and the woman in front of me was cleaning a headstone. The love, the bond doesn't die, that remains. If anything I think it gets stronger. All the little things that annoy us on a day-to-day basis, like leaving your dirty socks on the floor, not taking out the rubbish or leaving the toilet seat up, the small things that usually create cracks in a bond, they are deemed insignificant and unimportant when you experience a bereavement. There are no longer cracks, just a strong, reinforced bond that doesn't break, doesn't die and will remain forevermore.

In the past, I had heard that white butterflies and robins symbolised messages from lost loved ones to send gentle reminders that they were still with us. I remember seeing a robin on the fence in our garden when I was little, but since then I haven't seen a robin in about 20 years. And I can't remember ever seeing a white butterfly.

Guess what happened after we lost David... Yep. I would see white butterflies everywhere. At first, I thought it was a coincidence, but it was becoming too often and too convenient. I would see one when I felt down. I would see one when I was walking to school with the boys. One day one flew, at the same pace as my walk, next to my face for about a minute on the way home from shopping. I saw one merrily dance in the cemetery, weaving in and out of the headstones just loving and celebrating life. Even the boys started to notice how often we would see them. Every time I would see a butterfly I couldn't help but smile a little thank you to my brother who, I believed, was letting me know he was thinking of me as much as I was thinking about him.

Anyone who knows my mum knows that she **hates** butterflies. Seriously, she's terrified. As funny as it would be for us to watch, I'm sure she wouldn't appreciate a whole bunch of butterflies following her around. She did get a visit from another winged animal though. Yep. A robin took a liking to my mum's garden. Not just to her garden. To her. I'm serious, it made a point of always being around her. Almost terrorising her. I'm pretty sure small birds don't usually make a habit of dive bombing people, sitting a foot away and looking at you like 'what?' Sounds a lot like an annoying person who made a habit of terrorising us all with his sarcastic insults.

It makes me smile. It's funny. Just like the times that David would make comments about mum and dad quietly to me and we would be sniggering together in the corner.

You can believe in this or think I'm just seeing things because I want to. Maybe I am and if that's the case, so what? If a few butterflies and robin tormenting my mum make me smile and think of my brother, let me have that.

The most real and blatant experience I've had with my brother since his passing came completely unexpectedly. It's only ever happened the once and no matter how hard I try, I have not yet managed to experience it again.

One night, in the very early days after he died, I had just come out of the shower and was crying. Not an ugly cry, more of 'feeling numb but the tears won't stop' kind of cry. I was playing things over in my head.

Friday 13th.

Why?

They said he didn't feel anything, but did he? Did he know what was happening? Was he scared? Does he know how much we love him? Is he ok? Are you ok, David? I just want to know you're ok!

This is when the ugly crying started. I must have said "I just want to know you're ok" about 20 times. Ugly crying is exhausting. I knew this behaviour wasn't healthy or helping me. I was already tired from lack of sleep, ugly crying would have just made me feel worse. For one reason or another, something told me to meditate. Of course! Meditation shuts off your thoughts, ok good idea.

What I need right now is to stop thinking and get some sleep. If I can shut off my thoughts, I can stop thinking about all of this and try to get some rest. As I sat there, listening to my meditation music, I began to focus on my breath and started trying to focus my mind on nothing but my breath. Stop the thinking. Stop the questions.

But I just want to know he's ok. No, stop!

Breathe.

Breathe...

I kept my mind focused on my breath.

In.

Out.

I don't know how long I was meditating for. It couldn't have been more than 10 minutes, but I decided to release my emotions and the chatter in my head, and focus on my breath even if only for the time I was meditating. That's *if* I managed to focus at all. After all, all my problems weren't going anywhere. I could stress and ugly cry all I wanted after but right now I need to focus on my breath.

So I surrendered.

Then, something incredible happened.

Before I go into it, I want to tell you that I have no explanation. You can try to find a 'logical' explanation all you like, but I know, and I mean I KNOW it was real. I wasn't asleep. I didn't imagine it.

It. Happened.

So, I'm sitting on my bedroom floor meditating. I'm surprised by how well it's going and I'm allowing my focus to be on my breath and not on the chatter in my head. I'm grateful for the peace and rest my mind is having. Here's where it gets interesting. I don't remember a transition, I don't remember when or how it happened but I went from enjoying the stillness to suddenly realising I'm in a room (one I think I have seen before but thinking about it now, has no connection to this or to David at all). Anyway, there, in this room, was my big brother. Just me and him. I realise he's looking at me with a small smile but worried eyes. He was looking at me like he's worried about me. SNAP. Back to my bedroom floor.

I must have been with him for a total of about two seconds because as soon as I realised that I was looking at David it brought me out of the zone and instantly back to my bedroom. I opened my eyes and just said: "He's ok." It was half a statement, half amazement. Then I remembered my "*I just want to know you're ok*" ugly cry before my meditation. He found a way to tell me that he was. I could see it in his eyes. He was fine, just worried about me.

If anyone is thinking of meditating with the intention of seeing a loved one, I wouldn't recommend it. Since then, I have tried numerous times to have that experience again and it has never happened. I don't know if I want it too bad, if it only happened because I really needed it then or if it just doesn't work like that. As I said before, I don't have an explanation or answers. I can only tell you what happened.

This next bit isn't really about me seeing him. At least not visually. Since his death, I can think of three definite times when David has been with me. You can call this his spirit, his soul, but to me, it's just David. The most profound in my head was when my mum and dad went away a few months after he died. I was so happy that they went away because they deserved it. They needed a change of scenery, something positive to focus on and not be in a house that's a constant reminder of what happened to their son.

Anyway, I said I would go round and make sure there was no post left in their porch while they were away. As I went there one night, I remember being scared. Of what, I don't know but it's a big dark house and my brother had died there. I took the post in, and left, almost running back to my car. Thinking of it now, it's quite funny. I got in the car, heart racing slightly but happy to be leaving. As I put the key in the ignition, I stopped. I looked up and I knew. "*You're here aren't you*"? I instantly felt calm and the fear had gone. David was in the car with me. It was as if he sort of emotionally held my hand and told me not to be scared. I wasn't oblivious to the irony that he wouldn't have done that in real life. I laughed and probably called him a few names. I was talking to him, and within a minute or two I didn't feel him anymore. I carried on talking in the hope that he could still receive the message my words were carrying.

Many times, I have seen and heard things that I question if I had just imagined it or not. It's as if I know it's happening but I try to convince myself there's always a logical explanation. I always hear my TVs make a crack noise and for some reason or another, it makes me think of David. I have seen many movements, shadows and figures both in my house and other people's. It happens a lot and then I'm like a meerkat, standing to attention hoping that it's not a mouse.

After going to a spiritualist church, the guy told me "they're telling me to let you know you're not going crazy, it is them. You've been asking for signs and they're giving them to you." I thought I'd be freaked out by it, but all I feel is calm. When I feel David in my house, I'm not scared. The only way I can explain it is like when you're in a room and you know your child or another person has just walked into the room. They didn't startle you. Something in the air changes as if the frequency in the room alters. You just know they're there.

The most annoying, but funny, experience I have with my brother is that I hear him. **Constantly**. But it's not words of wisdom or encouraging advice or even sympathy. It's his insults and his one-liners. I've found myself voicing his words a lot since he died. I can hear him laughing and loving the fact that he can still insult us. Strangely, it comforts me. Even if it does feel like I have a mini David sitting on my shoulder, feeding me rude and offensive things to say to our family and friends. Sometimes I can't stop the words, other times I catch them just in time and tell myself they're his words not mine. *Sometimes*, I know what's coming out is a David phrase, I know I have time to stop it but I choose to let it come out, simply because it's funny. Times like that, I smirk inwardly as David and I snigger like naughty kids together.

As I'm writing this chapter, I'm stunned. I knew some things had happened to me. I knew they all happened to me but it's only when you write them all out that you see the true magnitude of how blessed I am to have so many connections that I have still linked to my brother. Thinking of all these lines of communication separately, you overlook so much. Now that I have a list of most of the things that happen to me, even I'm stunned.

My point throughout this chapter is that when someone dies, it's hard. It's painful. It's the most painful thing that I've ever had to go through. It's painful for yourself and it's painful to watch the people you love suffer too and, although there is nothing you can do to change what has happened, I really believe that if you open yourself up and accept that the way you communicated has gone but that you can find new and different ways to communicate, it will happen. Maybe not in the ways you want them to but things *will* start to happen. You just have to allow it to happen in its own way. The bond is there, stronger than ever. The memories are there. The relationship is still there. Can you think of a way for you to communicate to your loved one now?

Chapter 7
Finding God

"The wound is the place that the light enters you"
-Rumi

There will be a whole bunch of people who roll their eyes at the title. And I'm not here to judge you. Mainly because I *am* you. I was always amazed that people would 'find God' after a traumatic experience. Surely, this would make you question religion more? If there was a higher power, why would it take away good people? Why would it not end the lives of one of the many evil people on this planet? These are great questions and unfortunately, I don't have the answers to them. I'm also not about to tell you that I've 'found God'. I have a huge issue with that word. To me, It's too attached to an image of an old white man with a long beard sitting in the clouds chilling out. First of all 'God', the creator of the universe, the entity that birthed us all would definitely be female, if it had a gender at all, but that's just my opinion. I believe there is a big difference between being religious and being spiritual. You can be one, the other, both or neither.

Now, however, I can totally get it. Sometimes it takes a massive shock to the system for us to come out of the day-to-day trace that we live our lives. For us to appreciate the little things and see the world for the beauty it truly holds.

So here's my story. Something did happen to me. I found *something* but I can't give it a name because I don't really know what it is. Throughout my whole life, it had always been sitting there in the background giving me a wave now and again, but it was only when David died that it stood in my way and told me to sit down and listen.

My brother and I would have some pretty deep conversations about all sorts of things. The world, films, books, the government, family, friends, society and most definitely about food. Religion and spirituality would creep up now and again too. We were not raised in a religious household, our parents wanted us to go out into the world and make our own choices about what we believed and if we felt drawn to any faith. Something which I'm very grateful for. David and I were both of the belief that as long as you tried to be a good person in life, that was what mattered. It doesn't matter what faith or religion you believed in, if any. Just be a good person. If we all respect each others' beliefs and all try to be good human beings, surely, the world would be a better place.

I'm definitely no expert, but as far as I know, no holy book encourages us to harm our fellow man (or woman, or child), no matter what the media and extremists want us to believe. My brother and I would often talk about how we liked the idea of Buddhism and the more spiritual side of having a faith. *Karma* was a word that I always felt attracted to. Be good and good will be done onto you. Too often we 'take matters into our own hands' and react when we believe we have been wronged by someone. I believe let them dig their own grave and karma will teach them all the lessons they need to be better people. We can only control our own behaviour. If you try to control someone else's, you will not only fail but you will have wasted time and energy on an impossible task.

Just before he died, I was starting to learn about the law of Attraction. This is the idea that what you focus on, you attract into your life. If you research the Law of attraction, you will find a lot of famous and powerful people have utilised it to get to where they are today. People like Conor McGregor, Jim Carrey and Oprah. I don't know about you, but anything Oprah is passionate about definitely deserves my curiosity. The more I looked into it, the more I realised that so many people are using the law of attraction, even if they're not aware of it. People who say "I decided that I wasn't going to take no for an answer" so they worked hard, visualised and had their goal firmly planted in their mind. A lot of people talking about the law of attraction, talk about how they practised meditation and used it as part of their daily routines.

Now, meditation is something that has made an appearance numerous times during my life, usually by someone who I admire talking about it. When I was in college, my teacher introduced us to it first hand. She taught us the basics of meditation and how to clear our minds of the endless clutter and noise that we have become so familiar with that we hardly notice it anymore. Since then, I have tried to meditate now and again, usually once or twice a year to clear my head so I could fall asleep if I had too much on my mind. And I thought that's all it was, stopping the chat in your head as it definitely worked and it was great. Meditation is great for when you're so stressed out and need to detox your mind... but that's not all. Although this is one small part of meditation, I was yet to find out just how powerful, beautiful and valuable meditation practice can be on a daily basis, but especially when life has you backed against the wall.

In the days and weeks following my brother's death, I decided I would be open to anything that came my way or was suggested to me that could perhaps positively help me. I knew I was standing on a slippery slope and didn't want to slide down it. I wanted to climb to the top, even though going down would have been so much easier. So, when a good friend of mine suggested a book, I thought *"why not?"* And it did help a bit. It helped me to focus more on the positives and also look at the bigger picture. I am a mum to three wonderful boys and they deserve the best damn life that my husband and I can give them, so I had to try to find a way out of the darkness that was surrounding me.

I kept reading self-help or self-development books after the first one was suggested and found that it really helped to divert my attention away from the 'poor me' mentality to a bigger, wider world. It helped to expand my mind and really educated me on a lot of things. It seemed to be helping and I'm glad I decided to say yes when my friend suggested that book.

Yet, when a little voice inside me kept telling me to give meditation a try to clear my head, for some reason I always found an excuse. I would find something else to distract myself with and quiet the voice in my head. I had to get to my absolute lowest and cry my ugliest of ugly cries before I finally decided that I had had enough.

So one night, when my emotions would not remain locked inside anymore and wanted to be heard and erupted, I gave up. I gave in to the tears and to the voices and let it take over me. After a good hour of torturing myself. Going through all these scenarios in my mind about "*what actually happened?*", "*why did he die?*", "*Why him? He was a good person*", sitting on my bedroom floor, hugging my knees to my chest and rocking back and forth while pleading "*I just want to know you're ok. I just want to know you're ok! I hope you didn't suffer. I hope you didn't know what was happening. I just want to know you're ok!*"

It was an all consuming emotion and then that familiar voice calmly (and maybe a little bit smugly) said to me "You know this isn't helping you. I keep telling you what you have to do. Maybe you'll listen to me now?" I had had enough. I just wanted to silence my mind. I wanted to stop thinking. I think, if I'm honest with myself, I just wanted to forget even just for a minute. *Fine!* So I decided to finally give in and try to meditate. Just silence it all out. I just don't want to feel like this!

What happened next, though, was totally unexpected. I was blown away. Was seeing David due to the fact that I had no expectation for my meditation practice? Was it because it was exactly what I needed in that moment? Was it something else? I don't know. Honestly, I don't even care. It was beautiful. No actually, it was magical.

Since that night, meditation has played a major role in my life and I have seen beauty all around me. I'm well aware how this all sounds, but I can't help it. The more I meditate, the more I see beauty and life all around me. I have times when I let my emotions cloud my view, but I always try to recentre myself. It brings love and peace into my heart in a beautiful way. Whether you find that feeling through meditation, Judaism, Christianity, Islam, Hinduism, playing guitar or anything else, is irrelevant. I found that the conversations that David and I used to have were spot on. Just be a good person. Love your neighbour, love the Earth. How you choose to express that is totally your call. When have you felt that warm and calming feeling before? Can you recall how it feels now?

Chapter 8

Life Changing

"I can't change the direction of the wind, but I can adjust my sails to always reach my destination."

-Jimmy Dean

Everything about David's death pulled the rug from beneath my feet. There is so much that I never expected to happen. So much that I wasn't prepared for. I'm not only talking about the suddenness of his death but pretty much everything else that followed. You expect to miss the person, of course. You expect to miss their voice and their ways and the little things they say and do. And you absolutely do miss these things. You know your life is going to change because they were a big part of it.

I knew I'd miss my brother and our inside jokes and just the relationship we had. I'd miss his presence in my mum and dad's house and at any family get together we'd have. I also knew that probably, with time, things would be less raw and that I'd get stronger. After all, that's what everyone says, right? Although I don't know if you ever *'get over'* something like this. I think you just learn how to cope with it better as it becomes part of your life or part of your story. I don't think you can *'get over'* a trauma like that but you can learn to accept it and carry it as one of the many parts of your history that has shaped who you are today.

What caught me off guard most was more to do with myself. More specifically, my feelings and the voices in my head. Mental health is so important and we don't talk about it enough. Subconsciously, this makes us believe there is something wrong with us and that makes us feel so alone. It's painful and it makes you feel vulnerable but I'm going to be honest because someday, somewhere, someone might read this and think "*this is how I feel! I'm not alone after all.*" Because when you grieve, it's a very lonely place to be. You're already mourning the loss of a loved one and we can feel that separation so intensely that we can then sometimes distance ourselves from others while we deal with our pain, contributing even further to our loneliness. As I explained previously, I was surrounded by a sea of kind and caring family members and friends but I have never experienced loneliness like this before.

I would go through nearly every emotion known to man on a near daily basis. I would feel sadness, for obvious reasons, laugh at something my children said or something on the TV, then feel guilty for having the audacity to laugh at such a terrible time. I felt angry, at the world, at the injustice, at David. I was scared about what would happen to my mum and dad, to my sons, and then when we found out his cause of death might be hereditary, I was terrified for myself, my parents and for my children. I'd feel responsible, for David's health, for my parents. I'd want to be a daughter *and* a son to my mum and dad so they wouldn't feel so broken, so incomplete, but also want to run away as to not take his place.

I remember, my husband and I were clearing up at my parents' house and David's work trousers were hanging up, washed and ready to wear for his next shift at work. I took them down as I felt it was just another painful reminder of our loss, but mainly, of my parents' loss. I wanted to completely remove everything of David's so that my parents were not constantly reminded of what was missing but at the same time, I didn't want it to seem like I was removing him from existence because that was the last thing I wanted to do. I didn't want to be disrespectful to them, and I definitely didn't want to be disrespectful to David but I desperately wanted to fix things.

I was completely torn with every decision I was faced with. A lot of the time I felt totally defeated. How on earth do I deal with this? Running away was definitely something I'd contemplated a few times. I had no clue what to do or what to say, what to think or what to feel. I've said it before and I'll say it again, my husband was my absolute rock. He made a lot of decisions for me that I would have regretted, especially regarding our children. He kept a clear head to be the parent our children needed and was strong for me providing the support and love that I needed. Without him, I don't know how I could have found the emotional or physical strength to do anything. For a whole month, I was by my mum and dad's side every single day. Then, every single night I would either cry in Jamie's arms or be an empty vessel sitting on the sofa, my body was there, but I was in a whole other world. I really don't know how he coped so amazingly but I'll be forever grateful.

During the times when my mind went into overdrive, I'd sit and dwell on all the things that would not happen anymore. Going round my mum and dad's would never be the same. I used to love going there without my kids because I could just relax and talk to my mum, dad and brother which usually resulted in David making us all laugh. I don't think anyone can make me laugh like him, to the point of tears, doubled over and not being able to breathe. The kind of laugh where it's so intense that you're not even making a sound, until you finally take a gasp of air and manage to calm down, it pops in your mind again and you start laughing all over again.

You have memories like these, and you realise how precious they are and it makes you smile, and then the smile is followed by tears. Tears mourning for what will no longer be. As time is passing (and I'm working on myself and my mindset a **lot**), I am noticing that it's becoming more frequent that I am only focusing on the happy memory and how grateful I am to have it. The sadness is still there, but the tears don't come as frequently as they once did.

When we were little, we used to have joint birthday parties as our birthdays are just three days apart. We would invite our friends and family, there would be a table full of party food and we *always* had a bouncy castle. David and I were two years apart in age which, when you're a child feels so much, but even as kids, we were so close.

Our parties were always an event to look forward to for our family and although as we grew older, the parties stopped and then we wanted to celebrate individually with our friends in teenage years, we were always so excited for our birthdays. So for us, it was like Christmas. We would always ask each other what we wanted and what plans we had for our special day. The thought of not being able to do that again makes me sad and from now on, not only will his birthday be a sad time, I won't want to celebrate mine in the same way either. It almost feels disrespectful to him. The birthdays I fear the most are my 30th and my 31st. It has nothing to do with me being vain and in denial of getting older. It's that David was 30 when he died. On his 30th birthday, we were on a big family holiday cruising around the Mediterranean. It's a holiday that will always be bittersweet as I feel so blessed that we are able to treasure this holiday, but we were all blissfully ignorant to what would happen just two months later. My 30th birthday will not be as happy as it once could have been and then the thought of turning 31 and being older than my big brother is a very painful and uncomfortable feeling.

My husband and I alternate Christmases between our families. We decided this was the fairest way as you have to make compromises when you are both so close to your families. Yet, since David died, all I keep thinking is that I don't want my mum and dad to be alone on Christmas. I mean, they will never be alone in the literal sense, we have big families and always have at least 14 for Christmas dinner.

What I mean is that they won't have either of their children with them and this is when I have a battle with myself. I don't want to leave them.

But then I don't want to rock up to their house on Christmas day with my three children and let the chaos take over and make it all about me.

Or do they prefer that, the distraction? Maybe they want to be alone to quietly think about David.

Or maybe they desperately don't want to be alone but they are too nice to say anything and make me feel like they're guilt tripping me into something I don't want to do.

You see? Battling with myself. I have no idea what I'm doing. With this, with life or with parenting. Nine times out of ten I am having an argument in my head about what to do for the best. Ten times out of ten I question if I did the right thing. I spoke about this constant struggle in my head with the bereavement counsellor. She really put things into perspective for me when she told me to just stop. She told me to stop creating scenarios in my head. That I'm not a mind reader and unless I ask people, I will never know what they're thinking. She told me that we are all responsible for ourselves and our own happiness. That it is our responsibility to speak up if we feel we are being treated badly by a loved one and that by thinking the worst, not only was I blocking myself from feeling happy and free, I was almost putting words into their mouths. The moral of her story was, stop pretending you're a mind reader. Either ask the question you want answered or let it go.

When we found out the cause of his death, I wanted to find a way for me and my son Dane to try to do something positive as he was still struggling a bit. He was really into running and so I found a 5k run organised by a heart charity that, after speaking with him, I signed us up for. My cousin signed up too and together, the three of us raised over £1500. The whole family came to watch us run that day and it was so lovely to see everyone coming together, to support us, yes, but mainly to support David. It was a positive and a really great day. However, in the weeks before our run, I remember being in the car with my dad and he expressed his concern to me. Something I had never considered.

In between finding out David's cause of death, and getting the all clear ourselves, my dad confessed that he was apprehensive about me doing the run. He said he was proud of me for doing it and raising money for charity, but he feared for my health. He said, as we hadn't heard back from the hospital, he worried that if I had the same condition David had that it could trigger something in my heart. His words were "I've already lost one child, I don't want to lose you too". His words cut right through me but I assured him I would be fine and made a joke about me being like a bad smell and he can't get rid of me. Inside though, it cut me deep.

My point of all these little stories in this chapter is to show you how the simplest or most innocent thing has now changed for us. We think that grief will change our life by an obvious empty place at the dinner table, but it affects us in so many more ways. Sometimes it catches us completely off guard and other times it's that dreaded feeling in the pit of our stomach, knowing what's to come. There may be many occasions like this, or perhaps few. Either way, you just have to tackle it the same way as everything else, one step at a time.

I can't tell you when or if it'll ever stop, but try to reframe it. The reason you're so hurt is because that person is so important to you, even now. How lucky you are to have so many things that remind you of that person and your bond. How lucky you are to share that wonderful connection. One that not everyone is lucky enough to experience. And if I can just remind you, your bond is never broken. Everything else is just a case of readjusting. You will get there. Just take steps, no matter how small, just take steps to what feels good and what feels right. Be honest, be open and be patient. You **will** get there. Think of your loved one right now. Can you list three things about them that you're grateful for or appreciate?

Food for thought

"And if I asked you to name all the things that you love, how long would it take for you to name yourself?"

- Unknown

If there's anything my brother taught me, it's that we should all be unapologetic about who we truly are. David was never afraid to be himself. He didn't care if anyone called him different or if they didn't agree with his choices. He was always off doing whatever made him happy and never seemed phased by anyone else's opinions. I always envied this quality in him and now that I realise how short and precious life is, it's a quality that I am trying to adopt for myself.
I think we reach a certain point and realise that we have been living our lives for other people. We make decisions and life choices based on being scared that others will judge our decisions, or that we will be rejected because we're different so we don't take the opportunities that come our way because we don't want people to think we're leaving them behind. We're scared to grow and shine because we have encountered people in our past that try to knock down the platforms we build ourselves.

It would be so much more fulfilling if we allowed ourselves to be and do anything we felt compelled to. The fear of failure stops us from even trying, and the fear of death stops us from truly living. My brother's passing put a whole lot into perspective for me and it's unfortunate that I had to experience such a tragic loss to learn this, but as a result, I made the decision to live a life for both of us.

You hear all the time that those on their deathbeds say how they wished they'd taken more risks, cared less what others thought and been bolder. I don't want to wait until it's too late and then regret not living my life. I already have almost 30 years of things that I could have done a bit bolder and been more authentic by not caring what other people thought and been truer to myself. Maybe I could have achieved more, who knows? I do know that I'm not going to waste the next 30 and beyond.

My brother left before his life really got to take off, but he left so many wonderful and treasured memories and also some incredibly important lessons in his legacy. Let's all be a little more grateful for right now. Let's all look at the people we love and appreciate them while they're here, and tell them! Tell them why and how much we love them. Let's all take a few more risks and chances that could better our lives with an attitude of *why not?* Let's all be a little more honest about what makes us happy and who we really are. Let's all be kinder on ourselves and to others as we are all on our own journeys and dealing with our individual circumstances. And most of all, let's all be a little more like David. Let's all be more unapologetic about who we are and not pay attention to anyone who may have an issue. After all, the issue is theirs, leave them to deal with their own stuff, and you can have more energy to focus on your joy and remaining in your happy place, both inside and out. That in turn, will make the people around you and the world as a whole, a much better and enjoyable place.

You have as much right as anyone else and deserve to be as amazing as you can be. Everything in your life and everything you have experienced is part of your past and helped to contribute to the way you are, but it doesn't *define* who you are. You are special, you are majestic and you are deserving, the other small details are up to you to fill in. Start putting in the action to make your life amazing.

If you have days when you're happy, smile and laugh like a loon. If you have days of reflection and need to release, go ahead and ugly cry your heart out, but then get up, and follow your joy because you matter too. The world needs you to be as awesome as you can be to help inspire other people that can relate to you to be their most awesome self too.

So, my dear friend, it's time to spread your wings because hanging on the web does not do you any justice. You can come back and visit if you need to, but now it's time to take to the sky. Dance on the ceiling and shake your tail feather. Go forth and live your life. Simply surviving is not enough. A superstar lives inside of you and wants to come out to play. Your dreams are waiting for you to achieve them. Well…? What are you waiting for?

I wonder where your joy will take you?

Make Your Mark

Feel free to use this space to write down anything you like. Use it to release your emotions, plan an amazing activity for yourself, write a letter or even, to write a shopping list. Write whatever you need to and then you can rip it out and rip it up, if you want.

_____

_____

_____

_____

_____

_____

_____

_____

_____

_____

_____

_____

_____

_____

_____

_____

_____

_____

_____

_____

_____

_____

_____

_____

_____

_____

_____

_____

35319259R00063

Printed in Poland
by Amazon Fulfillment
Poland Sp. z o.o., Wrocław